SIMPLY AMOR

A Mother's Miracle—Living with Multiple Sclerosis

IRMA RESENDEZ

Published by:

Besos Publishing House
Rosemead, California
info@besospublishing.com
www.besospublishing.com

Cover design: Happy Planners LLC
First printing September 2014
978-0-615-99957-9
10987654321

For inquiries, contact: info@besospublishing.com

Preface

Each chapter highlights an insight or experiences that transpired during and after my diagnosis of multiple sclerosis. The titles for each chapter begin with the letters M and S. I have purposely defined what the letters M and S have symbolized for me.

Simply AMOR: Shares how love is within us and is expressed all over the place. Love is simply God giving us the foundation for faith, peace, unity, and healing that is rooted in love.

About the Author

The author's works, recognitions, awards and achievements are numerous, therefore, we have them listed on her website:

www.irmaresendez.com

Dedication

I dedicate ***Simply Amor*** to my husband Juan for his unconditional love, patience, and for standing by me all these years and my daughters Johnnie Nicole and Jacqueline for their dedication to making this world a better place. To my mother for always being there, and Papa Agustin for the delicious meals that he prepares for me; thank you especially for the special care and love that you give to my mom. Sister Jackie, I am grateful to you and love you so much for always being here and especially for continuing to remind me that you are the "the other mother to our girls - born from another." Thank you also to my brother-in-law & *Compadre* John Jauregui for the unspoken words that say, "I am here" and that show us that your love for the Resendez family is transparent. I love you too. Thank you Jonathan Jauregui, my brilliant young godson, for his innocence and heartfelt love for his Nina (me). I love your funny songs and great ideas of how we can better fundraise to help serve more people. Thank you to my sister Debbie and my brother-in-law & *Compadre* Rigo Tirado, I love you and thank you for being there when we needed you the most.

And lastly but not forgotten, My love to the many Familia Unida MS members, including also all who live with other medical conditions that continue to be courageous, amazing, and remind me each day that we all have a purpose and must continue to embrace each day with happiness, love and faith. You reinforce and bring to life the Familia Unida motto: **"You Are Not Alone"** (*No Estas Solo*).

Acknowledgments

$\mathscr{G}$reat friendships have been nourished and continue to flourish. I am thankful to all who have crossed my path and have shared a part of themselves with me to support others, as well as communities that benefited from our friendship and collaboration. Thank you for being in my life for a brief moment...or for a longer duration. I am especially delighted to highlight 14 Sheroes and Heroes that exemplify the meaning of friendships that are rooted in love, trust, and respect. I bet that I can write many inspiring stories about each and every one of them and give insight to the unique ways that they have blessed our diverse community and me. Muchas Gracias.

Irma Alfaro, a friend since seventh grade and who continues to remind me of why I had to finish my book and share it. Her unconditional love and the many years of friendship remind me that we all need to be surrounded by great friends.

Teresita Campo, a mother to Los Angeles who advocates for the underserved with a nurturing heart. Teresita is a mentor and friend who shares her wisdom and delicious meals. Her love is heartfelt. Definitely my shero and humanitarian!

Joseph Coria volunteers all that he can to many important causes. Joseph's sharing of his leadership and organizational development expertise builds healthy communities and has earned the respect from many for his heartfelt dedication to making a positive difference. .

Fernando Espuelas gave me the platform to have a voice, a genius in countless fields with values that are rooted in compassion to educate us on how to make informed choices about our rights and opportunities that are endless. Fernando brings awareness daily to social justice, equality, and civic rights to make this world a better place. I am honored to call him my friend.

David Damian Figueroa taught me to just do it and that's it! He showed me that we must not be afraid of the unknown. *Mi hermano* and hero is a creative innovator and humanitarian for all. David Damian demonstrates by his actions over and over again how one person can mobilize a community for goodness.

Jim Filipan gives love and support that is rooted by family tradition to his community. Jim's investment in others results in respect and countless relationships. Jimmy demonstrates that hard work and delegation to a strong trusted team increases successful outcomes, and he also blesses many with delicious meals from Stevens Steakhouse.

Dolores Huerta. Yes, she is the example that "yes, we can" (*sí, se puede*). Dolores is an icon and profound courageous civil and human rights beautiful spirit. She keeps reminding me "to keep going and going, to always be as you believe." She is a true blessing who always demonstrates that she cares about the future for all mankind. A shero loved from all over the world; I'm honored to call her my friend.

Zev Levy provides awareness to Familia Unida Living with MS in all places that he can so that more help is given to those in need. Zev has been a strong advocate and friend for many years and is always ready to help and share of his expertise to increase partnerships and support to our diverse community.

Diane Medina, is a dear friend, mentor, and confidante who exemplifies being a woman of integrity. Diane models making time for self, those you care about, and humanity. She is at the forefront of leading others to reach their goals. She is soft-spoken and is a gentle spirit visionary contributing to projects and diverse communities for a better today and tomorrow.

Adam Melendez gives love unconditionally with humility and all heart unselfishly. He never says no. A creative and quiet genius that is making a profound impact in lives and among strangers that he may never know. A guardian angel and protector of the vulnerable populations and pets, reaffirming that love is transformational. Adam exemplifies the meaning of a humanitarian.

Andy Padilla builds community and finds humor in all situations. Andy gives love that is contagious wherever he is. My spiritual advisor, my brother and friend forever is what we tell each other and know to be true. Andy inspires, motivates, and is an angel to many. He is a true blessing, and his dedication to improve and change lives and communities is admirable.

George Ramirez believed in me when I wasn't sure what to do and showed me how to write my first proposal. He has much expertise and shared it with love and kindness. He brought more friends and modeled leadership and is always keeping it real with funny stories and laughter... of course, reminding me that all is possible.

David Saperia, MD, for believing in me and encouraging me to start Familia Unida. I admire your dedication to your patients that is rooted in love and the inclusion of alternative treatments and medicine. Your smile is contagious!

Beth Zachary provided me with the proper tools and support to be healthier with love and respect so that I may be at my best. I admire her eloquence, patience, and friendship. Beth is a spiritual leader and a champion for health and wellness. An unexpected and beautiful gift of love that she gave to me that has forever improved my health and life. Thank you, Beth.

A special thank you to Dr. Rosie Milligan, nationally-acclaimed author, philanthropist and friend. Her expertise in many areas rooted in love, guided me with the completion of "Simply Amor."

Table of Contents

Introduction

$\mathscr{T}$he month of May was a fun month because my sisters and I looked forward to celebrating each other and our mom during Mother's Day. Our mom always reminded us that we didn't have to wait for Mother's Day to do so. On this particular year I had been so busy with the move out of our home to my mom's place while my home was undergoing a remodel. The construction to our home had caused us to temporarily move out of our house and move to my parents' home for 6 months. The construction was not going to be a distraction to this family's special holiday.

Our family is centralized by our traditions and even though Mom always told us to enjoy every day as "special"...we three sisters still followed our Mother's Day tradition and made this day *extra* special, as this celebration reunited us. My sister Jackie who was not a mommy yet also received gifts and cards from us because she was like a second mammie to my girls and a very special aunt to her nieces and nephews.

We usually got together for a brunch or family gathering. Thinking about how the construction would last way into summer, I was relieved for the early return back to my newly remodeled home! It was March, and we had moved back home, and now May construction and remodeling was almost complete. "Soon," Juan said, "our second-story addition will be ready for us to enjoy."

Mother's Day was almost here, and I hadn't had a chance to pick out the Mother's Day cards yet or find out where we would be getting together for brunch. . Oh great, I still hadn't made my appointment with my hairstylist to perm my hair. Hearing Gloria Estefan singing on the radio "I don't wanna lose you now, we're going get through somehow… if you want me I will be around forever… I pictured Gloria Estefan singing with her beautiful curly long hair. I would schedule my perm hairstyle just in time for Mothers Day. Maybe it will look as nice as my sister Jackie's perm that she had done earlier this year.

It was May of 1990 when the meaning of love for Juan and I would be tested. I was 28 years old, and our daughter Jacqueline was almost 3, and her sister Johnnie Nicole had just turned 4 years old in March. During that time I was a stay-at-home mom, a choice we mutually made because it was important for us that I spend as much time with them while they were young. We were on a tight budget but somehow we had figured out ways to enjoy family outings that were not very expensive, fun and educational. So, when the weekends were here, off we traveled to museums, walks at the Pasadena Rose bowl swap meet, the zoo and horseback riding at Griffith park was one of the girls favorite places to visit that ended with a picnic afterwards.

Chapter 1

Mother's Day Storm

*I*t was in the middle of the night. I was tossing and turning, and my body was full of sweat. My long black hair was still in a ponytail tied by one of Juan's black nylon socks. When I couldn't find a rubber band or scrunchie to tie my hair back, I grabbed one of his socks to hold back my hair in a ponytail, and it did the trick. Finally, my hair was away from my face and tied in a ponytail. For some reason, though, that night my hair tied back irritated me. I reached behind my head to untie the sock so that my hair could be free. Yes, now my head felt better.

I noticed that my hands were shaking and I felt cold, so I cuddled closer to Juan who was sleeping peacefully and was turned on his right side. I scooted closer to him so that my body would be closer to his back and I could warm up. I was still shivering, yet I felt hot while I pressed closer to Juan's cool back. I told myself, I must have the flu. I thought about all of the things I did that day that may have caused this. Maybe I felt horrible because I was outside sweeping without a sweater and it was chilly out that evening. My body ached. I just wanted to fall back asleep, but I couldn't. My mind was still racing. My stomach felt bloated too. Great, now I had to pee. As I turned to sit up, I realized that my body was weak. I was light-headed. I attempted to stand up from the mattress that was not on a frame but flat on the floor. I managed to sit up but was having difficulty with standing up. I just plopped back on the bed with my thoughts now focused on the difficulty I was having from trying to get up from the bed. I thought to myself...*I don't like this mattress. It's uncomfortable, old, too soft, and worn out. And it's on the floor.* I reminded myself that this was our temporary bed since our house was under construction and I didn't want a new mattress while all the dust was still in the air. I knew that soon we would be able to enjoy a new bed and our two-story house instead of the two-bedroom, one-story home. My mind began to wander some more as I lay in bed.

As I was reflecting all this, I still felt feverish. My body ached, and I was unable to fall back asleep. I was wide-awake now. It must have been around 3:00 a.m. It was very dark and quiet—so quiet that the only sound I heard was Juan's rhythmic breathing as he lay in a deep sleep beside me.

My thoughts took me to remember that Mother's Day was almost here. This Mother's Day I may have to spend it in bed. I felt like a bad storm of cold water had rushed throughout my hot body. Despite my fatigue, I could not fall asleep. I calculated after much thought that it had been almost 6 months ago that we had to move out from our home and temporarily live with my mom and stepdad, "Papa Agustin," so that the second-floor addition to our existing home could be completed.

I was glad that Juan and I and our daughters were back home, even though there was still so much work that needed to be completed inside the house. My body was cold, and yet, I was sweating as I continued to lie in bed next to Juan who continued to sleep soundly. My thoughts were focused on how the upstairs rooms were still not finished, and neither were the rooms downstairs. The dust was prevalent in every room despite the plastic that hung with gray or blue duct tape to keep the dust out of some of the rooms. The entrance to the stairs going upstairs was closed off to our girls and me as the construction team of Juan's friends worked with him throughout the day when he wasn't working at his regular job. The longer I lay on the mattress wide-awake, the hotter I felt and the more irritable I became.

The dust, the scrapped off paint that needed patching and new paint, cold floors and rooms without carpet that would soon be installed were thoughts that entered my mind as I tried to go back to sleep. The stairs that we now have that lead to a new upstairs were nicely framed and came out beautiful I thought. The fresh smell of wood would soon have carpet. It would look nice once the inside of the house was completely painted. The upstairs master bedroom still needed the bathroom to be finished. So much dust everywhere...a big mess because of the entire construction that was still going on. Soon, I thought, I would be able to enjoy the new upstairs addition. However, on this particular early dark morning, I could not sleep. I felt cold, my body ached, hot sweats and chills made me shiver, and lying on the uncomfortable old mattress didn't help. I felt so many emotions at once.

Despite my discomfort with the mess, I found comfort to know that Juan's vision of his dream house was coming true. Juan worked many extra hours at his regular heating and air-conditioning job to make ends meet and saved money so that we could continue with our home project. My body got more restless and feeling the urge to use the restroom was loud and clear now. It's so bad to hold it..."You know better" I scolded myself. Oh, how my thoughts distracted me.

I needed to get the strength to get out of bed to go to the restroom that was straight across from where I was lying. As I turned to sit up on the side of the mattress, I started to feel dizzy. I attempted again to stand, but my legs felt very weak. I had never felt like this before...I needed to make it to the bathroom soon since my sensation to pee was greater now and I felt my bladder very full. I looked toward my husband who was still lying on his side in a deep sleep and was no longer snoring. I would not wake him. He had been working with insulation, installing the new heating and air-conditioning system unit upstairs and coming home late from his regular work so that he could continue to pay for this home improvement project that was costing us more than we had anticipated. I thought about how good it felt to watch him frame the house alongside his carpentry friends. I thought of how happy Juan looked when he was showing our nephew Raymond all of his expertise related to construction.

Time goes by so quickly I thought as I remembered how when I was dating my now husband and my nephew Raymond was a little child chasing us at the park. Now my nephew was a young man in his early 20s. In reflection and now picturing them working alongside each other made me realize how fast time has, indeed, passed. My nephew was now a grown, handsome young man. It made me smile as I thought of how he looked up to his uncle Juanny (that's the name that he liked to call his uncle).

Thank goodness that all the walls were covered up with dry wall. A great deal of love and hard labor was going into remodeling this home, I thought. I took some pictures. I couldn't wait to develop them as that captured the before and after house. At least the outside of the house was done. Every aspect of this house was now built to Juan's specifications. Juan, a perfectionist, made sure that the octagonal window by the upstairs stairway was framed at exactly my eye level so that I could stand and see the mountains from the upstairs balcony and hallway.

I felt hot. I wanted to go back to sleep, but I couldn't. I thought the house was perfect before, but Juan insisted that he would build us a two-story home, so I supported his dream. Then in an instant, I was in touch with how horrible my body felt as I continued to lie in bed. My body was weak. I felt even more tired, and yet, my mind was racing with random thoughts, and I was feeling worse.

I tried to stand again, but I landed on my knees on the side of the bedroom carpet. I looked up to see if Juan heard me, but no, he was still sleeping...I was concerned now that I may pee on the carpet since I had been holding it for so long. "Are my legs asleep?" I asked myself. The fall knocked me right out of my current state of mind. My legs were weak and a tingly sensation traveled up and down them to my toes.

I managed to drag myself to the toilet by crawling on the floor. Good thing that the bedroom door and bathroom door were open and located straight across from me and not that far away. The night-light in the hallway allowed me to barely see the white toilet shadow that I figured was only seven steps away, or seven drags on my stomach away. I couldn't believe that I was crawling, pulling myself with my arms as my legs followed behind me. *Why am I crawling, pushing myself, dragging myself, and not walking?* I thought to myself. This felt like a dream. Was I half-asleep, or why did I feel so weird? Why was this happening? My body did not feel right.

The tile floor in the bathroom felt good on my stomach, so I lay there for a few seconds more before I pulled myself up to the toilet seat. I could finally pee I thought to myself. Oh my God, I made it without peeing on the floor. My bladder felt full...and yet no pee came out. Why can't I PEE! I was beginning to feel frustrated and more irritable. I began to cry and felt very emotional while my body felt hot. This feeling was not normal. Something was wrong, what was happening...I called out for Juan..."*Mijo...mijo...mijo,* come here!" He immediately heard me calling him. I saw him walking toward me, half-asleep, walking in a rush. There were no lights on other than the night-light down the hallway. It was dark...as he stood standing over me in just his underwear. He was looking at me confused as I sat on the toilet seat...He continued to look down at me, quiet for a brief moment, and just stood over me for a few seconds longer. I tearfully told him I didn't feel good. I want to pee but nothing comes out. My legs felt weird. I was exhausted. I just want to sleep.

Juan told me, "Your body is tired. You have been doing too much." He said, "I think you just slept on your side too long and it has caused your legs to fall asleep." He didn't know that I had crawled to the toilet, and I didn't think of telling him that at this very moment. He reached down to me, helped me up, and I grabbed on to his arm while we slowly made it back to bed, and no, I still had not peed. I felt like a drunk unable to balance myself. I was swaying from side to side, and my legs were not strong enough to stand by myself. I was hanging on to Juan. My entire body was holding and leaning on him. My legs were still weak, but somehow, I was able to make it back to bed with his assistance.

Once back in bed, I still couldn't sleep. My body felt achy, my legs weak, and my left hand felt like it was asleep. The tingly sensation was only for a few seconds at a time. It would come and go. It felt like my hand was asleep or when you fall asleep on your legs, and then your legs are trying to get back to the normal feeling, and they do after a few seconds. Well, that's the way my legs and left hand were feeling. I must have had the flu, and maybe this was the way a urinary infection felt like since I couldn't pee. This had never happened before. I felt bloated, tired, and irritable, but finally managed to fall into a light sleep.

I was awakened by Juan's kiss on my lips. It was now morning. Juan said, "You don't feel as hot anymore." I noticed that he was already in his work clothes and had overslept. "Stay in bed, just take it easy today,"

Juan said. "I got to go finish a job so that I can come back early and continue to pay for this remodeling project." I smiled and thought, *Yeah, right...How am I going to stay in bed all day with two little ones that will be waking up any minute now and will be full of nonstop energy?* As soon as I had that thought, our 2½-year-old daughter Jackie and barely 4-year-old daughter Johnnie Nicole were talking with each other in the next room. Juan gave me that smile like to say, "The thought was nice for a few minutes anyway."

Juan called out, "I will come home as soon as I can, and I will call you in a little while." I did not want to admit to him that I didn't want him to leave me. It was a strange feeling, but I still didn't listen to my gut. Instead, I told myself that I would feel better soon. I turned to my side and noticed that the answering machine light was still blinking and the number one appeared, reminding me that there was one message that was not retrieved. I forgot to play back the message from yesterday evening. I am almost certain it was my mom that called since we say goodnight every night and I did not call her yesterday. I would retrieve my message in a while. It was important, mom would call again, I thought.

Juan was off to work. I remained in bed and listened to Jackie saying to her sister in her deep, loud voice..."Sista, bring me my blankey," referring to her blanket. "Please, sista, please bring to me." I heard Johnnie Nicole answering her sister in her dainty, soft-spoken voice, "Yes, sister, I get for you." Then I heard Johnnie talking to her sister some more. Johnnie said, "Shister, why you always drop your blankey, ha, shister?" Johnnie Nicole asked her, "Ha, sista?" I heard them now in the hallway giggling and rushing and talking about who would get to Mama first.

They were now in my room, both standing over me. Jackie with her thick, messy, long, jet-black braided ponytail that I had combed the day before. Johnnie entered with her loose, messy brown hair. Her hair looked like it was teased, but I knew it wasn't. It was just the way it looked every morning. With one hand, she held her blanket that went everywhere with her. They both asked at the same time if they could watch their favorite morning television show with me. I smiled and told them that I could hardly wait to watch it with them. Jacqueline handed me the remote to the television that was nearby so that I could find the right channel. They joined me on my bed but quickly after doing so, Jackie jumped back off. She rushed quickly to her bedroom to retrieve her little blanket. Johnnie followed her sis Jackie, and now both were off my bed rushing together so that Jackie could retrieve her blanket. Both returned with their little blankets, and now Johnnie was also carrying her yellow container full of colorful toys that she snapped together to make buildings or people.

I wanted to be hopeful that within an hour I would get up and make breakfast for my girls and maybe once I ate, I would feel better despite not having an appetite, which was unusual for me. I felt totally exhausted, as if I had run 6 miles. I am not a runner, but I imagined that this is how I would feel if I did run 6 miles or more. My legs would be stronger soon was what I kept telling myself. This was the worst flu I had ever felt in my life. My body was telling me to slow down.

Jackie was now eating the string cheese that her sister had brought from the refrigerator. I thought how strong Johnnie's little delicate hands were as I pictured her opening the refrigerator. I watched Johnnie as she sat on my bed and separated the string cheese plastic for her sis. How smart that she already knew how to open the plastic and separate it from the string cheese. It made me want to smile, but I didn't. I felt horrible...

Jackie sat up with hungry eyes and said "Thank you, sista." Jackie peeled her string cheese carefully and slowly. She appeared amused by how she could peel little strands at a time that broke apart. Jackie was so concentrated on her string cheese while I was busy admiring her dark long beautiful hair and big brown eyes. Her eyelashes were long and thick. I saw my husband's features standing out in Jackie's face and her daddy's calm and serious demeanor.

Johnnie Nicole was sitting energetically next to me with a big happy smiley face. She was facing me and now eating a banana that she had just finished peeling. Our extended family seemed to think that Johnnie looked more like me. She had olive skin, and her features and personality that were more similar to mine. Although she was more like me by having a curiosity about her surroundings and smiling, she paid attention to details similar to her dad.

Johnnie showed off her creativity ready to give a hug while Jackie had a stronger resemblance to her daddy and took her time to observe you. Jacqueline was selective about whom she would hug. She was a critical thinker, listener, shy, dominant, yet sensitive, and thoughtful. She observed and enjoyed taking items apart and putting them back together.

Jackie is a sprinkle of her mama that was blended with her daddy. Both were unique, beautiful, and already evolving into their own personality with a little bit of Mama and Daddy and trying desperately to be like their sister. Johnnie trying to take items apart while Jacqueline had mastered this. Jacqueline wanting to follow in her sister's footsteps and speak out but preferred to watch better from a distance and behind her sister.

Both girls were now comfortable on my bed and both tried to feed me what they were eating. Jackie peeled a strand of string cheese and reached out to give it to me while Johnnie put her banana close to my mouth. I thanked them for wanting to share with me and told them that Mama was not hungry right now. My girls were still on my bed. The colorful plastic square building toys that were in different sizes and shapes were spread out all over the bed comforter. As I began to feel more tired, my girls were lying peacefully watching television, I closed my eyes...I smelled the banana peel on a napkin that was wrinkled up with the wrapper from the string cheese that was carefully wrapped and placed close to my pillow by one of the girls.

The phone ringing awakened me. I didn't know how long I had been asleep. I was startled and looked quickly to my side and reached out automatically to touch both girls that were asleep next to me. It was unusual for me to take naps, especially while Juan was not home. I NEVER slept while the children were up. It felt like maybe I dozed off a half hour. The girls were in a deep sleep, quietly wrapped in their blankets next to me. A commercial was playing on the television, and I could barely hear the phone that was ringing.

I reached for the phone. It was my mother. She asked me why my voice sounded like that. Her next question was, "Were you asleep? Are you sick?" she asked. I shared that I had a fever last night and that my body felt weak. She asked for Juan. "Is he home with you?" I shared that he had to go to work to finish a job. She made a sigh and sounded disturbed, and then continued her questions by asking about the girls...I told her that they were both fine and that both were at each side of me sleeping. I loved to hear my girls breathe when they slept. Their bodies wrapped close to me.

I told my mom that I would call her later...I didn't want to talk to anyone right now, especially her. I could sense that her next question would be, "Why didn't Juan drop off the girls with me if you were sick?"

I rushed to finish the call quickly so that she would stop asking me any more questions. I didn't feel like telling her that my legs were weak or that I crawled to the restroom. She was a worrier, and I didn't want to make a big deal out of nothing. Meanwhile, I heard the construction crew working outside by the bedroom window. There was noise also coming from upstairs. Hammers pounded and the electric drill sounds were very loud now. I just wanted silence, but it was not going to happen today. The crew was working on a timeline. I shouldn't complain. After all, I wanted our home to be ready soon. I had no idea that building a second story to our house would take so long. We were saving a lot on labor costs since Juan was skilled in many construction fields and his friends in various fields were giving us a break on their labor costs. Despite the savings, the cost was more than we had budgeted and was taking longer to be completed.

While I lay in bed with my girls, one of the construction workers walked past the hallway by my bedroom to use the downstairs restroom. Our eyes met, as he looked my way. I could feel that he was shocked to see me lying on my bed in my bedroom with my girls. He didn't expect to see me inside the house. I realized at that very moment that I was too weak to get up to close the door for privacy and my normal routine would have been to go to my mom's house while Juan and the others worked or I would be outdoors somewhere fun, away from the house with my girls while they worked. But not today, I could barely sit up.

I knew that Juan would come home soon because that is what he said before he rushed out this morning. I wished I had asked him to stay home instead. I wondered if he was working in Orange County or in West Los Angeles? He usually called me from a pay phone when he took his lunch break. I didn't pack him his lunch the night before and I was sure he would call soon to tell me what he had for lunch. Initially, I pictured him working on top of a roof of a building. However, I remembered vaguely that he mentioned that he would finish installing the air-conditioner unit at a residence in Huntington Beach. Since Juan's work was out in the field and not at an office, I never knew for sure where he was working until he shared his progress with me when he called me on his lunch break from the phone booth that he would find located close to wherever he worked. At around noon was the time that Juan liked to call me. Right before he enjoyed his lunch in his truck and in a shady area and before he read the daily newspaper. This was our usual routine most days when he knew I would be home and when it was convenient for him to call. On the days that I had plans away from home when he was away at work and on his lunch break, he still liked to call me and leave me messages on the answering machine so that I could listen to it when I returned home. He liked to share with me where he was enjoying his lunch and would describe the beach, the beautiful house near the mountain top or share what he read about that was interesting in the newspaper.

On that particular horrible day, it felt like it was past lunchtime. I was unclear of what time it was and I didn't feel like moving the clock radio to find out. My daily alarm clock that told me that Juan was home from a long day at work was the barking from our chubby black furry Chow-Chow dog Lad that was usually the first happy greeter at the gate. On this day, I was fuzzy and I was forcing myself to keep my eyes open and I didn't know for sure what time it was or if Juan was on his way home.

I knew that the guy that had passed by my bedroom was someone who had known my husband for years and was a good person too. I didn't feel scared, but I did feel uncomfortable that he saw me in my bedroom lying on my bed with my girls, feeling sick. I knew that if I were feeling good, I would have reminded the team of construction workers that we had cold water and refreshments in the refrigerator. Instead, the noise from those working disturbed me and made me more irritable. The noise was coming from all directions now.

I knew better, I knew that I would not be able to drive anywhere and that I had to stay in bed. I hoped that Juan would come home soon. After all, he did say he would come home early. How I wished I had the phone number to where he was working today so that I could relay a message to him. I guess I could have called his boss at the shop where he worked and possible his boss would be able to relay a message to him by going to the job site or calling the person where Juan was working and ask him to call me. Was I over reacting? Yes, I better not worry him. I convinced myself that soon I would hear Lad barking outside our house to tell me that Juan was opening the gate or was getting out of his truck that he parked inside our long driveway. I knew that he had a lot of work backed up and his boss was flexible knowing he had taken several weeks off in between work assignments so that he could continue to work at home. We had bills to pay, and I didn't want to further delay his work nor accept how sick I was feeling. My eyes felt weak. I closed them while the girls lay sleeping on each side of me.

I didn't recall what time it was. I opened my eyes to see that my mother and sister Jackie were standing over me as they awakened us from our sleep. My mom was upset because she said I was burning up with a fever and said that my face was pale/yellow and that I looked horrible. She couldn't believe that Juan left to work with me in this condition. I guess my fever came back because I was not this hot when he left for work. They both began to pull me up. My sister got some sweatpants out for me and helped to get me ready because they said I was going to the hospital now. Mom would stay with the girls while my sister drove me to the hospital. My sister told me that Juan had just called and was on his way.

It took both my mom and sister to hold me up and position me in the front seat of my sister's car. My mother yelled at me all the way to the car because she thought that I should have been transported via ambulance, but I refused. She said that my legs were not strong, and I disagreed and told her that I could walk if I held on to both of them. My car seat was positioned all the way back while my sister transported me to the community emergency hospital. I awakened when I heard my sister Jackie yelling out for a wheelchair.

The team of doctors could not figure out what was wrong with me. I was given a codeine prescription for my body aches and headache and other medication for nausea and dizziness. The doctor told me that I should feel better in a few days. He ended the quick conversation by saying, "You are doing too much. Your body is just exhausted." I was told to go home and rest, and if my condition with my legs worsens to return. My legs were weak, and I was only able to walk by holding onto someone or the wall. I agreed to return if I got worse. I wanted to go home, and, yes, my body was tired.

On the way back home, my sister had to pull over twice because I had to throw up on the side of the street. I felt everything moving rather quickly and the dizziness felt worse. I just want to sleep. My sister looked scared as I became disoriented and confused. She kept saying that she could not believe that the doctor at the emergency hospital had sent me home. I reminded her, "Sis, it's OK. Remember, we don't have health insurance anymore. I will be better once I lie down on my bed." My sis told me that she talked to Mom on the pay phone while I was at the emergency room. She was frustrated because she had to wait in a long line to use the pay phone and the lady before her talked and talked for a long time despite the long line of people waiting patiently for their turn. Finally, my sister took a deep breath and said that Johnnie and Jackie were having a delicious meal that Grandma prepared and that Juan was home now. I still had no appetite and couldn't seem to hold down any food. My stomach was upset, and the dizziness persisted.

A few days passed, and again, in the middle of the night, I was awakened by aches throughout my body. My fever had returned. I noticed that my legs felt weaker. This time I was not afraid to tell Juan to please take me back to the local community hospital. I felt horrible.

My sister was on her way to our home to stay with the girls. I dozed off as Juan drove me to the hospital. This time, the doctor on call made the decision to have me transferred by ambulance from the Community Hospital to the county hospital. My mother accompanied me in the ambulance. I knew this because she later shared this with me, not because I remembered it. While in the ambulance I could barely hear the siren. I could feel that we were traveling fast. I was wearing an oxygen mask and quickly fell into a deep sleep. I was awakened abruptly and saw by my surroundings that we had arrived at the county hospital.

A person wearing a white jacket asked me, "What is your full name?" I answered "Irma Resendez." The next question was, "What year is it?" I thought for a moment, and then replied, "1990." The next question was, "What day is it?" I replied, "I don't know." That was followed by, "How old are you?" I thought for a while, then responded correctly and said that I was 28 years old.

Soon, another person came to see me who identified himself and said he was from the neurology department. He helped me to sit up on the gurney. He explained that he was about to poke my legs with a safety pin. I gave him a look to show him that I did not want to be poked with a safety pin. But despite my uneasiness I said okay. He began to poke my legs with the safety pin. I was watching him, but I didn't feel the needle going into my legs as he poked it in different areas. He proceeded to poke at the bottom of my feet. First, he poked one leg. Then he poked the other leg. I was watching now with my eyes wide open because I couldn't believe that I could not feel the safety pin enter my feet. I could see the safety pin enter my skin, but there was no reaction from my legs, nor did I feel any pain as it entered my feet or legs. Then he poked again, and this time I saw little red blood spots because the safety pin went deeper into my skin. He wiped the red blood spots with an alcohol wipe. He moved toward my feet area and poked the bottom of my feet again. My feet didn't move and did not react to his poking at all. He poked my inner thighs, and I could barely feel the jab from the pin.

The doctor than asked me to walk toward him. I looked at him. His name badge said his name was David Saperia, Neurology Department. I told him, "Dr. Saperia, I don't want to fall again." I was remembering when I tried to get out of bed the other night and landed on the floor.

He said to me with his concerned eyes and a big smile "Don't worry. I will catch you. Just try to walk to me." He then stood right in front of me. As I began to position myself to get off the gurney by putting my feet on the floor, my legs felt a tingle feeling, like when they fall asleep. I was about to hit the floor when Dr. Saperia caught me right before my knees touched the ground.

"Your legs are like noodles!" he said.

The next thing I remembered was that I was rushed away on a gurney. My eyes felt heavy. I could barely keep them open. I could not see clearly. My vision was blurry. It remained blurry for a moment;

then again I was able to focus. Then it was blurry again. This feeling of blurriness, and then being able to focus came and went. Moving fast while on the gurney made me dizzy even with my eyes closed. I felt horrible with each movement. I began to also feel anxious. I could feel my heart racing. I wondered where my husband was since he didn't go with me in the ambulance. As soon as I thought that, I could see that he had just entered the room. I felt better knowing that my husband was there now. He reached out to me and kissed me on my forehead. I could see that his eyes had a look of confusion and were watery, but he didn't want to cry in front of me.

So much was going on at once. People were talking fast, and now I was traveling even faster on a gurney. Yes, I could make out his face... Juan was walking fast alongside the gurney. He looked scared, helpless, and was speechless. He appeared to be in disbelief and in total shock. His blank face had no expression other than fear in his big brown eyes. Juan remained silent.

As I was rushed even faster on the gurney, I quickly glanced to my other side and recognized the voice. It was my brother-in-law Rigo saying, "Don't worry, *Comadre* (sister-in-law), you are going to be okay." I could hear the uncertainty in my *compadre's* (brother-in-law) voice, like he was not sure of what he just said. He didn't sound convinced that I was going to be okay. I was unable to look at his face as I closed my eyes again thinking that the dizziness would go away, but it didn't. I tried to comprehend what was happening. Was it the speed that was making me dizzy? Why did I feel light-headed? I didn't know. Juan was not talking, but I knew he was near.

I keep thinking, *why can't I feel my legs?* Everything looked blurry again. I was unable to focus on the face of the man in the white coat rushing alongside the gurney or remember what they were all saying.

I was confused. This was not happening I kept thinking to myself. I wanted to wake up from this nightmare, but I knew that this was no nightmare.

I felt the doors swing wide open and heard them close behind us. My husband was no longer by my side. I could barely hear a woman's voice walking away and telling my husband that he couldn't be in the x-ray room and for him to please wait in the waiting area. At that point, I immediately wanted to know where my girls were. I said as loud as I could, "Wait, please tell me, where are my girls? Who is watching my girls?" A friendly woman's voice said, "Don't worry, try to rest now. Your girls are fine."

"Where are my girls? Please tell me who is watching my girls."

She no longer responded. I realized at that moment that Juan had taken me to the emergency hospital. But then Mom was with me in the ambulance. Nothing made sense. I was disoriented. How many days had passed? I didn't know if it was morning or night. The girls did not come with us. Did Juan call someone to stay with them? Was my sister with them? I didn't know. "Please, God, help me," I prayed. I was scared. I wanted to go home to my girls. They would wonder where I went. I did not tell them I was going to the hospital. They were asleep in the middle of the night. *Was it night? When did Juan bring me? Who brought me?* I didn't remember seeing my sister or Mom or know who was with the girls. I felt anxious, as I couldn't remember these important details. I didn't want my girls to wake up and go to my bed and discover that I was not there. I had never been away from them, not even for one day. I had to go home soon and put them to bed when the day becomes night and say their prayers with them like I do every night. Tears rolled down my cheeks. I could feel that my heartbeat was beating fast.

I was told that they were going to have x-rays done now. I overheard discussion of other tests that would follow. I felt cold under the white sheets and thin white blanket. The x-ray room was dark, very quiet, and I felt like I was far away from everyone else. Why was this happening? I couldn't feel my legs or my toes as I tried to move them. I heard conversations at a distance. They were checking to see about a space for "Resendez" in the intensive care unit.

"Changes and crisis transpire every day around us, and when the change or crisis affect you or a loved one, a new feeling is awakened."
Simply Amor

Chapter 2

My Silence—Intensive Care Unit

I was in a deep sleep when I was awakened by several voices talking to each other in a low voice all around me. I tried to open my eyes, but they felt heavy and wouldn't open. I wanted to speak, but nothing came out of my mouth. I made out the voices, even though I could not see anyone. It was my husband, Mom, and sister Jackie. They were discussing who would help Juan watch my daughters while Juan worked. I heard Juan respond to my mom that he would stay with the girls at her house. He continued by saying to my mom, "Or you could come and stay at our house," then the conversation turned to possibly one daughter could stay with my parents and my other daughter would stay with Juan's parents. Juan was saying that he would continue to go to work, and from work he would go stay wherever the girls were.

I tried again to open my eyes, but I couldn't. My eyes simply would not open. They felt heavy. I tried to speak, but I wasn't able to put into words what I wanted to say. They couldn't see that I was trying to speak or open my eyes because if they did, they would stop all this nonsense and listen to me. I wanted to scream out and tell them how upset I was.

How dare they talk about my girls being separated and going to different homes? I wanted to shout out, "No, no one will take care of my girls. I will be home soon." How could they even think about separating them?

My sister Jackie, I felt, was reading my mind. She finally said, "No, I don't think that we should separate Johnnie and Jacqueline." She continued by saying in a firm and louder tone that she would pick them up on Thursday evenings and take both sisters back to my mom's house on Sunday night. Juan then said that he would stay with them at my mom's house, and then said that he would go to work from there. My mind wanted to get in this conversation, but for some reason, I was unable to speak my thoughts. It was as if I was very far away from them and they couldn't see that I was awake listening to their every word. I recall telling myself, *why is no one asking me what I want for my girls? Don't they know that I am lying right by them as they speak around me in their whispers that are now louder than whispers?* I felt so weak. Was it the medication that caused this reaction? I didn't know. All I knew was that I was unable to respond to their conversations, and I felt my heart racing.

I finally opened my eyes. My vision was blurred at first. Then the conversations stopped. I was able to focus, and, yes, I wasn't dreaming. This was real. I saw that my mom and sister were crying. Juan said nothing. He just looked at me with his big brown sad watery eyes. He said softly, "Don't worry, the girls are okay, and their grandpa is with them right now" (referring to my stepfather).

I responded, "Please don't separate them. They are very close, and it will be horrible if they cannot be together. (Johnnie Nicole and Jacqueline were 15 months apart.) You cannot separate our girls." I was tired and fell back asleep.

It felt like it was in the middle of the night or very early in the morning when a person wearing a lab coat was standing over me. He had a friendly face. He identified himself as my nurse. He explained to me that I was in the intensive care unit. He was a nice-looking middle-aged black man. He appeared to be friendly and concerned. I immediately noticed the IV and other tubes in my body. I asked him, "What's wrong with me? Why can't I feel my legs?"

He responded, "Don't worry. Your doctor will see you in the morning." He gently told me to go back to sleep. I felt exhausted and weak and fought to keep my eyes open, but I just couldn't. I was so tired. I was wondering when I would go home. I missed my girls. What was wrong with my legs? Would I be able to go home soon? I dozed off in a deep sleep.

"Uncertainty at an unfamiliar place brought family unity." Simply Love

Chapter 3

My Scary Experience—Strangers in the Night

$\mathcal{I}$t seemed liked just a few hours had passed when another patient was brought in to my room at the intensive care unit (ICU). The patient entering my room was a young Latino male, possibly in his late 20s, with tattoos covering both arms and more tattoo writing in big letters covered his neck and side of his head. He was cussing loud in English and in Spanish. He was expressing loudly how mad he was in extremely vulgar words. He was angry because he was handcuffed to the gurney and screaming that he was in a lot of pain. My curtain was opened and his bed was placed directly across from me. I noticed immediately that his hands and feet were tied up with silver chains that had a thick leather trim around his hands and feet that were attached to the silver chains. He was forcing his body away from the bed. He was yelling, trying to break away and free his hands and feet that were tightly secured against the silver metal gurney.

He scared me as I witnessed him getting more out of control as he realized that he could not free himself. I noticed the bloodstains on the side of his sheet near his stomach area. He appeared to be injured. He soon became more furious and aggressive. I was afraid that he would break loose and hurt someone despite his injury. He was strong!

Our eyes meet for a few seconds. His eyes looked angry or evil, and I felt his negative energy. It brought chills throughout my body, and, yes, he terrified me. I immediately turned away. I became more worried as I overheard the hospital staff discuss that he would go to the county jail once his condition stabilized.

My curtain was closed shut by the nurse on call now. I think she saw my body language that may have showed fear and being very uncomfortable. Finally, I wouldn't see what was happening, and he couldn't see me. Minutes passed and the yelling and cursing finally stopped. I believed that he was given a sedative to sleep because there was no more screaming, and now I could only hear the machine that was making noise from the left side of the bed of another male patient who lay on my left side.

I fell asleep despite my resistance. I had told myself that I would stay awake since I feared sleeping in the room with this unstable person that scared me, who lay in a bed across from me. I perceived him as violent or dangerous, especially if he was chained up and tried to break loose. I wondered what happened to him to cause him to be so out of control and angry. Eventually, I dozed off, and when I awakened the next morning he was gone.

I dozed back to sleep and during a deep sleep, I was awakened again and told that I would be having a spinal tap done in a few minutes. I was unfamiliar with this procedure. I asked the soft-spoken short man wearing a white jacket, "Why? What does this mean? What are you going to do?"

He replied in an orderly fashion as if he had answered these questions many times, "I am an anesthesiologist" and identified himself by his name. He continued by explaining that he would be taking out some liquid from my spinal cord and that I must not move when this procedure was in progress. He showed me the very long needle that appeared to be over 5 inches long. He shared that this exam would help to determine what was happening inside my body. He asked me to get in a fetal position. I had my back toward him, lying on my right side facing the wall. Soon after following his instructions, I felt the big long needle go in my spine. I screamed from the top of my lungs. A sound I had never heard came out of me. This was a painful procedure that was even more painful than when I gave birth to my daughters. This pain caused me to lose my breath as I tried to keep still. He reminded me that if I moved, the needle could move into a wrong place and that I could become paralyzed permanently. I later recalled that I had skimmed quickly through the consent forms that I signed that took away any liability from the hospital for doing this procedure. I was frightened and sweating. I screamed like never before in my life. The pain was so profound that it felt like I had stopped breathing. I screamed even louder as I felt the needle move again...and again...and again. I cried out, pleading for him to stop. I told him that the pain was too much. I screamed again, "Please stop. I cannot not take this anymore!"

He kept saying softly, "I am almost done," and moved the box with tubes to show me the many little clear tubes that he was filling up with the liquid that he was taking from my spinal area. The liquid was clear. I could not believe that I was going through this. The procedure was so painful, and the big needle in my back hurt so much. This was the most pain that I had ever felt in my life.

I heard my screams echoing in the hallway. Toward the end of this procedure I felt like I was going to faint and thought I would pass out at any moment. Finally, he finished and asked me to lie in the opposite direction and toward my left side. I was instructed not to move from that new position for at least 4 hours or else I would have the worst pounding headache ever or be dizzy and that may cause me to get nauseated and vomit. He said again that I must now turn facing the left side of my bed.

I slowly moved to lie on my left side. He reminded me again that I must stay in that position for at least 4 hours. I listened to his instructions and lay facing the left side of my bed staring at the white curtain. During my stay at this hospital, I had two spinal taps. Recently, I was informed by others who had spinal taps done that when this procedure was done to them, they were given preventative pain medication (pain killers) when they had their spinal tap. They also expressed that they felt minimum or no pain at all when they had that procedure done. I was not given any pain medication and don't understand why I had to endure that pain. I now wondered if the reason that I was not given pain medication was due to the fact that I did not have medical insurance. Did the nurse forget to give it to me? Did the doctor forget to write the prescription? Why wasn't my family informed about this? Why did no one come to talk to me about this? I had no answers, just confusion as I tried to lie as still as possible, alone with my thoughts. All I know for sure was that this was painful.

Another day passed. I was disoriented. My eyes began to focus on the middle-aged Latina woman who was weeping uncontrollably. She was standing on the left side of my bed. My back and head hurt if I tried to turn to my right side. As I lay still recovering from the spinal tap I could only see her back. I could see that her entire body was shaking, especially her shoulders. She was looking down at a man on the bed next to me. His body was still. I didn't hear the machines that I had been hearing the previous days as he moaned day and night. Her crying became louder interspersed with painful moans. The woman's cries were now out of control mixed with yelling. Two hospital staff members went to comfort her. She was still standing just a few steps from my bed facing the man that lay silent on my left side.

There were a total of three beds on each side of the intensive care unit where I was assigned. To my right there was no one in the empty bed space. My bed was located in the middle, and now the man who moaned throughout the night was silent. The only moans now were coming from this sad woman. No more machines were making noises by his side. I only heard the suffering of the woman next to him. It was easy to lose track of time when I was in the intensive care unit.

The minutes seemed like hours, and hours felt like days. I told myself that I would also be out of control if I stayed here any longer. I was already vulnerable, sad, and did not feel comfortable in my new surroundings. My bed was in the middle of three beds on the immediate left side when you enter the room. On my left side lay silent the man who lay in pain since I had arrived. Straight across from me were three more beds with three more male patients that came, but male patients always occupied the beds.

I was not familiar with the many emotions and thoughts that entered my head. My head still hurt, and I felt fuzzy from the spinal tap. I was not aware if it was morning or night. I reflected again on the man that lay just a few feet from me. I realized that I had never heard the man speak. The only sounds that came from him were moans until his final breath. The day before was the last time that I heard his moans and the sounds of the machines that were connected to him. These machines sounded like they were pumping something in and out and were on all day and night, working nonstop.

The other day when they did the spinal tap I had to lean on my left side as I recovered. I was facing his bed and did not move for over 4 hours. My bed was just a few feet from his. I tried to keep my eyes closed because I did not like facing his bed. The curtains were closed shut most of the time. In earlier days I could see and hear the noise of something hitting the silver bedpan that was placed right near his bedside close enough for me to see. It was blood. Yes, blood was dripping onto the bedpan. Even though I tried to keep my eyes closed shut I could still see the blood dripping into a silver urinal pan that was at my eyesight on the floor below his bed. From the first day I arrived I had noticed it. That bedpan had been placed at the same spot. The moaning man that had been making the same sound nonstop since I had arrived now lay silent.

The other day when the anesthesiologist had instructed me to lie on my left side after he completed the spinal tap procedure, I wanted to turn away to my right side and face the wall instead. I did not like facing where the man in pain was. Why didn't the anesthesiologist tell me to stay facing the right side and face the wall? Did it matter? It was too late to ask. He had left and was gone. I followed his instructions and turned in the opposite direction and lay in pain for over 4 hours, facing the man who moaned and moaned in pain and in the direction of where the bloody bedpan was. I didn't want to risk messing up my body any further by trying to move in the other direction, away from the bloody bedpan. Even, if I wanted to move, I couldn't. My back was in so much pain. Any movement increased the pain that I felt in my back and in my head. The nurses continued to check on me and advised me not to turn on the other side and advised me not to move or lay on my back because the pain would be worse.

The cold pack on my head didn't help the horrible headache. Any movement would increase my dizziness and headache. I shut my eyes tight again and prayed in silence. I asked God why all this was happening. I asked God if I was also going to die in this room. I tried to escape by making myself believe that I was no longer in this room. I pretended that I had jumped out of bed and was no longer there and that this was just a dream—no—nightmare! I fantasized that my girls were in my bed back home and that we were eating string cheese and drinking cold chocolate milk. But the unbearable hospital smell reminded me that I was still in the hospital. How I wished to escape.

The man that had lay in the space next to me was now dead. Just like that. On the morning of his death, I managed to look up and made eye contact with the young male nurse who came to close my curtain completely. Before he did, I had a glance of the white sheet and white knitted blanket that nicely covered almost all of the now peaceful man's upper body. I was not able to see his face. The curtain didn't allow for me to see his entire body. *Rest in peace,* I thought to myself. *No more suffering for you.*

I wanted to remember as much as I could about that person. I tried to figure out what his face was like since I only saw parts of his body that lay next to me. I remembered his right arm was dark skinned, similar to my husband. The fragile woman had cried so much. Her love had just passed away. Maybe that was her husband or her boyfriend. I was not able to give her eye contact. She was at a side view, and her back was to me. She was a petite lady wearing light jeans and had a long sleeve light blue shirt tucked in. By then, the male nurse had already fully closed my curtain. As the woman continued to cry I felt her pain expressed by her sounds and from her tone when she spoke. She sounded and appeared to be in her early or mid-thirties. Her cries were painful and consistent.

A few more minutes had gone by, and more people were talking all at once. I closed my eyes again. I didn't want to hear this anymore. I imagined for a quick second how I would feel if my husband or loved one died. No, I didn't want to feel this kind of pain. I just wanted to go home. Tears rolled down my cheeks as I could feel her pain. She prayed in Spanish. "*Padre nuestro que estas en el cielo . . .*" (Our Father who art in heaven)...

Then I heard the noises of the bed being lowered. I heard the many footsteps rushing out at the same time, and I heard the wheels of the gurney pass by. The sad lady followed out and kept repeating the same words, "*Te quiero mucho mi amor, te quiero mucho mi amor*" (I love you very much, my love, I love you very much, my love). I felt an immediate sadness as tears continued to run down my face. It didn't matter that I didn't know him. My tears were real, and I couldn't keep myself from crying.

The nurse who brought me more medication interrupted my thoughts. She reminded me that the prednisone would help me and might make my body swell up because it was a steroid. She told me that another blood test, and CT scan, and MRI were being scheduled. I felt numb. My body was already weak. Now my soul felt like it had gone somewhere far from me. I spoke to God, not out loud but in my private thoughts. I confided to God that I was afraid and that I didn't want to die. I pleaded, "Please don't let me die. I want to see my girls grow up." I wondered why the doctors wouldn't allow them to visit me. It's been almost 2 weeks since I was admitted to the ICU and I still hadn't seen my girls. Can I give them this illness or disease? I don't want to harm them or anyone. Maybe I should stop requesting for them to see me while I am still under observation and they still didn't know what I had, or at least no one has told me. I heard the nurses tell my family that I could not receive flowers while in the ICU. Would the flowers or plants die too, like the man next to me? Were we so infected with contamination and contagious? I had so many questions and yet still no clarity because the test results were still not clear. The nurses advised me that when my doctor comes to see me tomorrow I should ask her all my questions and that she would tell me what she knew.

How I missed Juan and my daughters. I wondered what they were doing. Juan had come to see me but was only permitted to stay for a few minutes at a time. He looked overwhelmed the night before and didn't express how he was doing. He just wanted to know what the doctors had told me. He avoided talking about his feelings. I hadn't heard my girls' voices in weeks. I craved them. I couldn't keep them out of my thoughts. I needed to see them now. Lying in that bed for days at a time gave me much time for my thoughts to wander in many directions. I didn't feel well and not knowing what was going on with my body or unsure of what the MRI would show kept me in anticipation and made me restless.

It broke my heart that my girls were not permitted to visit me. I still didn't want to know how much this hospital stay was going to cost us. The whispers echoed said that Resendez would be here for a while. I couldn't think that far in advance. I needed to know now if what I had was contagious. Why wouldn't anyone tell me why my body felt so weak? My vision was not blurry anymore, but I was not able to get out of that bed. I had no control of my bladder or bowel movements; I used a bedpan and had a catheter connected to me so that I could urinate and release the urine in a pouch. I hadn't been able to poop either. Maybe it was because of all the fluids and not eating much yet. A male nurse would give me a sponge bath. Why was my body too weak that I couldn't get up and take a shower or bath?

The team of doctors came by again with the medical residents. Groups of three or four doctors stood around me with several resident doctor students to discuss my case. More than three or four doctors and their students circled around my bed to ask the same questions and poked me some more. They took turns poking at my legs and arms. I saw tiny spots of blood come out again as groups of interns continued to wake me and poked me with safety pins and wiped off the tiny blood spots that were caused by the needles going into my legs and feet. I didn't feel the poking, but it started to annoy me that more students came around to ask the same questions that were just asked the day before by other resident students. I finally said no to the various groups of students who wanted to poke me again or who wanted to do an interview assessment.

As I look back, I asked myself, why didn't I request a female nurse to bathe me when I knew how uncomfortable I felt to have a stranger, a male, no less, bathe me. Up until being in that hospital, Juan was the only man who had ever touched my body with a sponge. Why didn't I say no sooner to the different groups of student residents who kept coming by to do one more interview or assessment? I felt like I was an animal in a cage, looking at the clock tick minutes and waiting for Juan to come to visit me for brief moments. This routine group study by students and doctors felt like I was a "project" and not a person. I gave them permission every time they asked until I finally became disturbed when awakened again while sleeping.

I asked myself, why was I in ICU with only male patients? Was this because I had no health insurance, or was this a common practice? Does this practice continue today?

Another day passed. I was awakened again during the very early morning and late at night for more blood tests, IV changes, and more x-rays. The man that was at my left since I had arrived was now gone. His bed was made up neatly. New pillowcases and new sheets were placed on the empty bed. No evidence of the bloody bedpan that was on the floor a day earlier. A person had passed away in that space next to me. The next patient would soon occupy the bed. How, before that day, did I not ever wonder who had lay in the bed that I was currently lying on? How many more went home or had passed away in the bed that I now occupied? I wondered. There was so much that I hadn't thought about until I had witnessed a stranger leaving this earth or transported to the county jail or simply was gone when I woke up.

By now, almost 2 weeks had passed. I was told again that my daughters could not come to see me while I was in the ICU, especially until they figured out what was wrong with me. I got it. I understood and realized that the hospital was trying to protect my young girls from whatever I had. I prayed that I did not have a deadly illness or a contagious disease. The agony of being away from my family was worse than not knowing what was happening to me.

As time went on, it was more difficult for me to not have contact with my daughters. The last time they saw me was the night before I was admitted and when they woke up the next day, Mama was gone. I pleaded with the doctor and head nurses that I needed to see my daughters if only for a few minutes when I learned that Jacqueline (she was 2½ years old) was not eating well and was distant and sad. Johnnie, I heard, was wetting the bed. This was unusual since Johnnie was 4 years old and was potty trained by age 1 and didn't wet the bed or use a diaper since that time. I felt guilty and saddened that they, like me, were going through a stressful change and their tiny bodies were reacting to our separation. Possibly, my girls were feeling the emotions that everyone around them was feeling and were trying to cope too.

The following morning my male nurse came to me with a smile on his face and said, "Guess who's coming to see you this afternoon?" I responded in a flat voice, "The neurologist? The student residents?" He said, "Nope, your daughters!!! However, they can only come for a few minutes." This special day was one that I will forever remember like it was yesterday. This moment was so vivid and yet so long ago.

My Jacqueline stood by the door with a white mask and green doctor gown, and her shoes were covered in the paper cover slippers. The top scrub was the type that was used by doctors going into surgery. The green shirt was long and fit her like a dress. Johnnie was also wearing a white mask, and the identical green shirt that also fit her like a dress, and the puffy paper shoes were tied so that they were not loose and covered their shoes. The nurses provided them doctor scrubs, orientation, and together, with their dad, had already washed their hands and arms and were sanitized before entering is what I learned afterward. At first they were just standing at the door quietly observing Mama. Then big sister Johnnie pulled her sister all the way inside the room. They began to tiptoe to me since they noticed others in the room were sleeping. They quietly walked toward me, looking like miniature doctors.

They looked so precious as I watched them walk quietly and excitedly toward me. As they tiptoed forward I glanced at their daddy, well groomed as always, hair neat and fully shaved. But his eyes were so serious and sad at first glance, then turned to joy as he studied the girls' reaction and eagerness to come to me. No one spoke at first. Finally they reached me and saw that my eyes were watching them in excitement. They ran and jumped up onto my bed and cuddled me so tight, as if saying, "What is happening, Mama? We miss you." Daddy was watching their every move in complete silence and walked slowly and quietly behind them. Jacqueline, with her beautiful big brown eyes, was staring and was trying to absorb everything in sight displayed around her. Her eyes had dark circles under them, and her face looked thinner than the last time I saw her at home. This concerned me because I had never seen her eyes like that. I thought of when my sister Jackie had told me that Jacqueline wasn't eating or sleeping well. I held my *mija* Jacqueline close to me.

Jacqueline had a flat affect look on her face. She was amazed and shocked by the long tubes and machines that surrounded me. Maybe it was because of the bruises on my arms caused by the needles. My left hand by my fingers had recent bruises from the butterfly-type IV tube. The front of my right foot had bruises from needle poking as they had done a lot of blood work; therefore, I had bruises in different places.

Johnnie told me with excitement that she was her sister's little mommy while Mama was in the hospital. I thanked Johnnie for being such a good big sister and little mommy as well. Jacqueline didn't say much; she listened as her sister spoke. Jacqueline studied the room and soon she focused all her attention on me and grabbed onto me closer as she cuddled me until she was completely on top of me. Johnnie asked, "Mama, when are you coming home?" Johnnie seemed to take the role of wanting to give me good news too. She was smiling and talking fast as she shared that grandma gave her and her sister baths with Jergens cream again, and then asked me to smell her. I agreed with her that she smelled delicious.

Johnnie began to share that her Nina (my sister Jackie) goes to pick her and her sister up, and then they stay at Nina's house and go to Burger King and eat French toast, and then they go to the park and to the beach. They eat ice cream and play fun games. Johnnie was talking so quickly trying to remember everything she has done since she last saw me at home. She talked about how she and her sis slept together in one bed at Grandma and Grandpa's house.

Her facial expression turned to sadness when she described that sometimes she and her sister cried for me, but they covered their mouths tight so Grandma wouldn't hear. They didn't want Grandma to get sad if she saw them crying, and then Grandma would cry too. Johnnie told me that she and her sister would cry together in bed, and she would hold her sister tight at night until she fell asleep. She added that sometimes they wet the bed, and as soon as that happened, they would take off the wet sheets from the bed and lay them on the carpet by the side of the bed and in morning, "Guess what, Mama? The pee was all gone!"

All the time Johnnie was talking fast, Jacqueline was still silent and in a daze, not taking part in this conversation. Instead, Jacqueline put her hands over my hair gently and touched my face, as if to check if I was really her mama. All Jacqueline wanted to do was feel me and bring my face closer to her so she could watch my every word expressed.

Their visit was too short and lasted no more than 15 quick minutes. I wanted them to stay longer, but the nurse came back to say, "So sorry to interrupt but your family needs to leave now." I knew it was time for them to leave as it was said to me many times that children were not allowed in the ICU. I was grateful that I was able to see them and hold them if only for a few minutes. As they were preparing to leave I told them, "Mama has to stay here a little bit longer to get better soon." I then reached above my bed shelf for a beautiful white stuffed animal bear that my sister-in-law Norma had brought me when she visited from San Diego. I gave the white cuddly bear to Jacqueline. I told her as she grabbed it quickly and held on to it that this soft bear was called "Little Mommy." I asked her to take care of it, to hug it, to sleep with it, and to cry with it if she needed to. I asked her to remember that Mama loved her very much and so does everyone that is taking turns watching her and her sister while Daddy has to go to work and Mama has to get better.

My girls began to cry quietly (they were considerate of others in the room who were sleeping or lying in silence). Jacqueline said in her sweet deep whispers, "Mommie, we don't want to go. Why can't we stay with

48

you?" Johnnie then said (pointing to the side of the bed), "See, Mama, sister can sleep right here and me right there" (referring to each side of my bed). I looked up at Juan, and I could see that his eyes were swelling up with tears and was seconds from breaking down. He immediately picked up the girls and carried them out. I wanted to cry, scream, and run out as fast as I could. My heart was racing inside. However, I sat up without saying a word and closed my eyes. It was too painful to watch him leave with each girl carried in his arms. I showed no tears, and he did not make any more eye contact with me after he kissed me. I couldn't keep my eyes closed long because I had to see them one more time. So I opened my eyes quickly and called out "Mama loves you" and gave them the biggest smile I could make. I blew them more kisses and said again, "Mama will see you soon," and repeated again, "Mama loves you"...until they were out of my sight.

Four weeks had passed. I still hadn't gotten accustomed to using a catheter to urinate. I despised having a bowel movement in a bedpan but that was better than defecating in a diaper or having accidents on the bed due to my current limited mobility. God bless the nurses, and especially the nurse's assistant, who, in my opinion, had one of the hardest jobs in the ICU. It was a humbling feeling when I had to rely on others to assist me with my private and intimate personal care. I was confined to my bed while in the ICU. I longed for a shower or a bath by myself, in private. I did not want to be there. The hours continued to feel like days, and the weeks felt like months.

After a few days shy from a month at the county hospital, one of the neurologists informed me that I would be transferred to a rehabilitation hospital for continued care in the following days.

I felt an emptiness and uncertainty leaving the county hospital because the neurologist and the team of doctors were not able to confirm what my diagnosis was. The only words that they kept telling me were that I might never walk again.

I was in disbelief that from one day to the next my life would never be the same. I was supposed to spend Mother's Day with my family and my mother. We were supposed to get dressed up in our colorful flower dresses, eat delicious food, exchange gifts and sentimental cards, and be in conflict as to where we were going to have brunch. I was supposed to get a hair perm. For a brief moment, I thought of the lyrics again from Gloria Estefan that now were not just some words that I sang along too but instead deep and meaningful words that triggered an array of emotions, "I don't want to lose you now, we're going to to get through somehow... No, I didn't want to think of my relationship with Juan right now. It was easier to picture myself having mothers day brunch and exchanging gifts with my sisters and mom. I wanted to scream but couldn't scream. They would think I was nuts! Besides, the nurses had to deal with so many difficult patients already. I did not want to be one of them. I really liked the nurses and the staff. They were nice, and it wasn't their fault I was there. I had to be reasonable and strong and go with the flow despite the uncertainty that I felt. However, when I recalled everything that had transpired that led up to this, I still was in disbelief. One day I am walking, and the following day I was not. I wasn't involved in an accident, hadn't broken a leg or fell. Whatever this was that was causing this shutdown in my body was in control. I felt out of control, and I wanted my body back. I wanted to pee and poop like I did before. I didn't want to use a bedpan or have a diaper as my options. Or worse, not be able to tell when I had to go to the bathroom and have an accident in bed. This thing that no one seems to know or want to tell me what it is made me dizzy, made my eyes get blurry without warning, took away the strength in my left hand in an instant. Why did this have to happen to my left hand? I am left-handed and I didn't want to scribble again and be forced to write with my right hand like when I was a child in grade school and told by some teachers that only "stupid kids" wrote with their left hand. I need my left hand to get stronger, and I don't want to drop my cup with water again because I forgot to use my right hand. How was I going to take my girls to the zoo if I did not have strength in my legs? So much time to think about...What if, or what is to come next, or what is to become of me? My marriage? My daughters?

I reflected on the various tests done while being a patient here. The milligram, CT scan, breathing test, blood test and spinal taps. For sure, I would never forget the spinal taps. The doctors stated that the MRIs showed that I had inflammation and lesions in my brain and inflammation on my spinal cord. I felt numb, speechless, and scared, and wanted to hold my girls and sleep with Juan and make love to him.

Dr. Saperia checked in on me regularly and demonstrated heartfelt compassion. My stay at the county hospital lasted a month. A total of 2 weeks in the intensive care unit .The other 2 weeks I was a patient in the second-level intensive care unit where Juan and my daughters and family were allowed to visit.

The nurse on call at the county gathered my "get well soon" and "I miss you cards" and put them neatly in a white bag and placed it on the side of the gurney. She also tied my balloons on my left side of the gurney and all of the nurses that cared for me made sure they said good-bye before the end of their shift, an unexpected and nice gesture that meant a lot. Those that had cared for me that month and were present on the day that I was being transferred to the rehabilitation center also came by and wished me farewell. I had an opportunity to thank them for their care. I knew that I would probably never see them again, or at least that was my private thought. I wanted to forget this place and wished it were only a bad dream. However, at the same time, I felt like I was leaving a group of friends that I had known for a long time and felt thankful for them. There was something to be said about relationships developing faster when you are in close quarters, and especially when you are depending on others to care for you. Even though I was only there a month, the time spent with them was very personal.

Having a stranger wash my hair, bathe me, clean out my bedpan, and attend to my personal hygiene was uncomfortable at first. However, in a strange way, I adapted to them and this new environment. I needed them, and they did a good job in letting me know that it was their job to care for me. They often expressed that they didn't feel weird doing all the tasks that were required when you are a nurse or a nursing assistant.

I had the opportunity to get familiar with the nurses and team in the ICU on a personal level too. Many shared insights of their personal background and what they liked to do when they were off work. Some shared why they became nurses or doctors and told me where they liked to go eat good Mexican food nearby or which restaurants were the ones they avoided.

What I remembered the most from my stay at the county hospital was how well the nurses had interacted with each other. They did not take their job too seriously that they didn't know how to have fun. They knew when it was time to be serious and took appropriate action to a variety of situations on a daily basis. They found reasons to laugh despite the bleak situations that surrounded them each and every day. They knew when it was time to take their nurse role to professionalism and also when to be silly and find humor in the daily experiences that came to be. I felt very grateful for their care and humor that they brought to me and among each other, despite the ongoing turmoil that was witnessed in the intensive care unit (ICU).

While I was being pushed down the hallway on the gurney at the county hospital to the ambulance that was waiting for me downstairs I could feel the breeze on my body and blowing through my hair. I inhaled the faint smell of hospital food, medications, and that peculiar unpleasant scent that was familiar in hospitals. I felt a sense of relief leaving this place, even though I knew I was being transported to another hospital. Maybe it was because I was no longer in the intensive care unit where death was evident for some. I was glad that I was finally being transferred to a rehabilitation center in a nearby city.

While I lay flat on the gurney with my colorful balloons that were blowing in all directions, some partly deflated, I smiled as I began to reflect on the support from my family. I remembered when each of the balloons was brought to me and who brought it. I thought of the white fluffy teddy bear that I gave to my *mija* Jacqueline and how serious she looked as she held on to it tight with one hand and how the other hand was locked with her sister Johnnie's hand before they were carried out by their daddy.

I pictured their beautiful tiny faces with looks of confusion and sadness as they left my room along with their dad who rushed out with them as fast as he could. I smiled as I remembered Johnnie Nicole looking so grown up, talking fast, clear, and soft-spoken as she took on the role of the big sister at age 4.

I thought of hearing the nurses telling my family that balloons were not permitted in the ICU and how happy it was to finally be in the lower ICU unit where balloons were permitted. The only item that was allowed to be in my area in the initial ICU was the teddy bear that I gave to Jacqueline. I was content to learn that Jackie took her Little Mama white bear everywhere she went. She was sleeping and eating better after seeing me that day in my hospital bed and returning again when I was moved to the lower ICU unit.

How quickly our life could be changed in an instant and how quickly those that came to visit were able to make time for family and friends. Yes, their daily routine or planned tasks were put off when I was faced with an emergency or a crisis of possibly not having this opportunity at a later time. It felt good to see those that I loved and was surprised to see some family members and friends that I hadn't seen for a while. Before this hospital stay I saw my family and friends but only in busy walks and conversations, not really talking about real issues because we thought, "Yes, we can catch up another time." Then unexpected tragedy hit home and now we somehow made time to say, "I am here," or "I love you and proclaim that you are not alone." How comforting it was to have this opportunity to witness those I loved demonstrate what comes naturally when faced with a crisis.

I began to think again about my daughters and wondered who was with them now. I missed them so much, and I reminded myself of what one of the doctors told me. She said, "At the rehabilitation hospital, your family can visit and see you every day, and there is a park area with picnic tables and a grassy area for your daughters to run and play around in."

My daydreaming was interrupted when the gurney stopped at the elevator. The paramedics and I waited for the elevator to open its door when the neurologist, David Saperia, came rushing down the hallway and stopped at my gurney. With a big smile on his face he watched me being pushed into the elevator. "Don't worry, Irma. One day you will walk again, and I want the first dance, OK?"

I looked straight at him, as I lay surrounded by my colorful, somewhat deflated, balloons. The only words that came out of my mouth were "Okay." My mood was sad, but I thought afterward that it was nice of him to say that we would dance one day when I walked again. He was a gentle spirit who demonstrated genuine concern and compassion for his patients. I tried to picture us dancing, but found it hard to believe it. This neurologist was someone I admired. I had the time to observe his interaction when he conducted his rounds and checked in with his patients that shared the room with me. The ability to see or hear other conversations and interactions a few feet from me was often unavoidable, especially with only a curtain separating us from one another just a few feet away. That curtain afforded us the only privacy whatsoever. Therefore, I could hear all conversations and most whispers as well.

What I wanted to know right at that moment was: What was happening to my body? Why did my legs feel like noodles? Would I walk again? Would I die from this? What's going on with my brain? So many tests done...Will my husband be able to care for the girls the way I would? Were my girls okay? Will my husband be able to do this? I even questioned if, in fact, he would want to remain being my husband. Yes, of course, he would stay. I began to answer my own questions. Yes, he loves his girls; he loves me, I reassured myself. However, another thought came in my head: Would he still love me if I were unable to walk? Would he still want to be with me if we are not sexually active? Would he leave and give up on us? Has he already? Could I blame him if he left? I noticed that he couldn't seem to talk about any of this.

So far, Juan was not showing me any emotions, other than trying to hide his fear and sadness. He was not communicating what he was going through. Instead, he focused on sharing updates about the girls and who had sent their regards. He hardly spoke about what he was going through, and Juan avoided those questions by asking me more questions instead. He didn't seem to be able to process this. Could it just be because he knew that the patients right next to me in this shared space were listening, and he wanted more privacy?

Juan looked tired; he looked so exhausted when I saw him the night before. Juan, my *mijo*, was probably not sleeping well either. Who was he sharing his feelings with? He doesn't reach out much to anyone. Juan had few close friends and was such a private person. His family, his girls, and I were the ones with whom he spoke. Maybe my sister or his brothers and both of our extended families were supporting him right now. He hadn't shared anything about his work with me. I realized that I forgot to ask him about his jobs and how that was going. How were we going to pay for all these medical bills? I thought again, I missed him so much. I wanted to go home. I wanted to make sure he was okay and that we were okay. I didn't know for sure. So many questions unanswered.

What I didn't know before protected me from questions that I had now, now that I did know of life changes and death. My questions now were: How do we address the injustice of quality of care when there were so many questions that need answers? Where do we begin to improve or address these disparities? How safe or acceptable is it for females and males to share space in the intensive care unit or hospital room? Should patients with a violent history or unstable behavior, or worse, patients that were being transported to the county jail, share a room with patients who are fragile, nonviolent, and of a different gender?

These are tricky questions because when I was in this situation, it didn't really faze me so much what was happening around me most of the time because there was so much I was dealing with, dealing with myself. I had never before been in a hospital, and this new experience sparked new awareness, questions, and ideas. I ponder the reasons now years later why I shared a room with only men in the ICU. I rationalize it to be because possibly there was no other space available and their care was just as urgent as mine and possibly life-threatening. I knew already that hospitals had limited funding, and that translated to limited or inappropriate ICU space, overcrowding, lack of health insurance, and does this translate to less options and a lower quality of care? I was grateful to learn that my hospital bills were covered in part by medi-cal with a share of cost that Juan covered. In the near future, I also qualified for Medicare due to permanent chronic illness diagnosis that will be shared soon.

Today, I still believe that patients' rights need to be more comprehensive and implemented clearly for the patient and their family, accompanied by a long list of dos and don'ts. They should be informed of examples of what is considered a violation of the patient, the patient's care, and their rights, because often, the patient is not in his or her right state of mind to read or comprehend what is transpiring due to the urgency of attention because of the illness, pain, injury, or shock that is experienced. Not only does the patient experience these hardships, but the family members as well who are dealing with the current crisis or incident that keeps their mind preoccupied with dedicating their time to be with their loved one. Therefore, they are not aware of or have been informed to the fullest of the patient's rights. However, if a pamphlet or appropriate materials are given to family members, especially in a manner that is culturally and linguistically available (written in clear and appropriate language), more families would know how to advocate for themselves and their loved ones. Having more of these resources would not only be educational, but would also empower the public, which would reinforce appropriate health and public policy practices.

"Strangers provided care and acts of kindness to strangers, to me...thank you." Simply Amor

Chapter 4

My Speedy Ride via Ambulance

$\mathcal{O}$n a cool, clear day I was transferred from my bed to a gurney that would travel with me to the rehabilitation hospital. On my ride in the ambulance, I thought again of the death of a patient who had lay a few feet from me. The emotions that occur when injury, pain, illness, and separation from those you love due to sickness could make you feel helpless and empty and give you a sense of being vulnerable when others are responsible for you that you don't even know. Wanting to trust that these people were doing their best for me was an unusual sensation, especially seeing that not all patients were getting the care they deserved, mainly because the needs were so great, with many patients to attend to. The language barriers were evident, as well. Not enough attention for all...Was this an impossibility? Were my expectations too high? I pondered how my hospital stay would have been if I had the financial resources to pick any hospital in the world...If I could afford a better hospital where there were enough rooms to separate the women from the men.

Despite all the thoughts running through my mind about the difficult experiences I had at the county hospital, I tried to look on the bright side. I thought of how my experience would have been much more difficult if I didn't speak English and if I didn't have the support of my family and friends. Even though I was disappointed with certain aspects of my hospital experience, I remembered that this county facility was known as one of the top training schools and medical facilities for many researchers and prominent doctors that served all over the world. At least the treatments that were given to me were of exceptional quality.

I wanted to leave my sadness at the county hospital and leave on a positive note. However, the mixed feelings and emotions were so great and unclear. I carried all these thoughts with me as I traveled in the ambulance to the rehabilitation center.

My mind began to wander again. Could I be brave and not let my uncertainty and fear keep me in this state of panic that creeps up on me every so often? I constantly questioned myself, "Can I do this? Is my faith being tested?" I hadn't prayed as much as I did now and found comfort when I did. "I don't know what is happening to me" were the reoccurring words that I kept thinking while I rested in this room and tried to be brave. There is still so much I didn't know.

I dozed off to sleep and was awakened by the ambulance doors being opened quickly and feeling the cool air that rushed throughout my body. I was still wearing the oxygen mask and realized that we had already arrived at the rehabilitation center. I was rolled from my gurney into a room where there were three beds on each side of the wall facing each other. I noticed two empty bed spaces and was immediately transferred in the middle bed between the two female patients that seemed to already be expecting me. The beds were located in similar close quarters like before. When I saw that all the patients in the beds were women, I gave a sigh of relief. I did not want to share my room with men again. I quickly stopped myself from remembering the uncomfortable experiences that

I felt when I shared a room with all men who were either gravely ill or that gave me the eye glare making me feel like I was being undressed. The new place appeared like a more relaxed atmosphere, but that wasn't entirely the case. The unpleasant smell that I thought I left behind at the county hospital had penetrated in the walls and in the air at this rehabilitation center. It smelled just like the county hospital that I had just come from.

As I entered the hospital room, I soon learned about the ladies that occupied the beds. They were made up of different cultures: Mexican, black, and white. All were watching me from their beds and welcomed me almost immediately. A few sat up in their bed as I felt their eyes observing every move as the nurse and medical staff transferred me from gurney to bed. I looked up at my surroundings, and one lady gave me eye contact and a faint smile. Another said, "Hello, good afternoon" (*buenas tardes*) in Spanish, and then turned her back away to give me privacy.

As soon as the medical staff left the room the ladies from their beds began asking me questions. They did not hold back. The questions began almost immediately. They were curious to learn about me. All of them shared in an orderly fashion why they were there, some in Spanish and others in English.

A young African American girl in her early twenties shared that she had eight multiple gunshot wounds throughout her entire body and brain. This incident was a result of a drive-by shooting that left her extremely paralyzed. In one area of her body she still had a bullet lodged because it was much too dangerous to remove it. The long metal sticks that supported her head looked painful and heavy. I didn't recall what the purpose was of the metal box-shaped outline with long metal sticks, but she referred to them as pins. It appeared to give her balance and strength as it was positioned on her shoulders and screwed or attached somehow to her head.

She slowly sat up higher in her bed. With great difficulty, she showed me some of the scars and the location in her chest area where there was still a bullet. I was shocked to learn about all she had gone through at such a young age and to know that a bullet was still inside her body. I thought to myself what a miracle to learn that after all those gunshots to her body and head she was alive and able to talk about what happened to her. Her speech was slurred, and I could tell that she had difficulty speaking and her strength appeared frail. I immediately liked her. I thought despite all of this, she was able to find humor and said with a faint smile, "Most of the bullets are gone. Only one souvenir still inside me." Her voice had a tone of someone who could be silly and outgoing.

A Mexican woman in her late forties tearfully said in Spanish that she was in a fatal car accident where a drunk driver killed her youngest son. She was crying as she repeated again that her heart was broken in many pieces. As a result of the accident, she was now paralyzed from her lower extremities and was suffering from brain trauma. She said she was taking medication for her depression as she found it difficult to want to live. She ended her thoughts by sharing that the pain of losing a child was worse than the brain trauma and paralysis she incurred.

An elderly Caucasian lady shared that she had fallen again, breaking her hip and hitting her head, resulting in a brain injury. On top of all of that, she was recently diagnosed with cancer. The lady was unable to walk, and her pain and moans at night reminded me of similar moans that were shared by the other patient at the county hospital.

A younger Caucasian lady in her early thirties had short blond hair, spoke fast, and appeared to have a psychological disorder as well. I based this upon her behavior because she was repetitive, anxious, and unable to concentrate, causing her to not make a lot of sense. Maybe it wasn't psychological; maybe it was all that pain medication that she had to take to calm her down. She screamed and shared that she "saw things and people" all around her, especially when she didn't take her medication. Her bed was located to my immediate right side. She wore a cast covering most of her body and expressed pain and itching that kept her from sleeping. Yes, I suppose a cast covering most of your body would give a person a reason to scream.

All of these women had some sort of trauma to their brain and had injury or illness that caused them to be paralyzed or to have limited mobility. A neurologist was seeing us all. They were eager to want to know my background and history, and especially what happened to me. One asked me, "Were you in a car accident like me? What happened to your legs? Did you ever walk before? What's wrong with you?"

My stay at the rehabilitation center was a totally different experience from that at the county hospital. The main difference was that while I was a patient at the county, I was in the intensive care unit and was dealing with disbelief, shock, and uncertainty of whether I was going to die like the man that lay next to me while I was there. I was too depressed or despondent to carry a conversation with the patients like the men that lay next to me and shared the ICU with me. While at the ICU, we were all in our own world dealing with our own urgent situation, sleeping, or were awaken for more medication or personal care. Besides, there were multiple men coming and going. It was more of an emergency and critical setting. I never thought of speaking to them; I could barely deal with myself.

Arriving at the rehabilitation center was a sign that I was going to get better because it was not an ICU; rather, it was a rehabilitation center. It seemed like a more peaceful atmosphere, despite not knowing yet what my diagnosis was and sleeping next to a person who I believed to be psychotic. She rarely slept and kept us up at night because of her loud conversations that she had with herself and the invisible people she claimed were mean to her.

My diagnosis was still a mystery during the first month of stay at the rehabilitation center. It was clear to all of the medical team that I was experiencing some kind of a neurological disorder that needed more attention. The MRI, x-rays, and CT scans of my brain and spine showed evidence of lesions and inflammation. They also showed abnormal activity that was evident on my spinal cord. I continued with the treatment of prednisone (steroids) and the muscle relaxers that helped with the pain that sometimes traveled from my head to my toes. I was told that the traveling pain throughout my body was called spasms.

The ladies that shared the room with me had critical health issues, but I felt like I would be able to sleep better here. I did not feel threatened by the women in the room. Even the one that talked all night, she didn't seem harmful to others. She was just in her own world, and other times she was present with us. Her personality was always more relaxed and pleasant when she was taking her medication.

This facility did have grassy areas as described by the doctor at the previous hospital. I was no longer in an emergency ICU setting at this facility. However, it was evident that my roommates had serious trauma to their brains and were experiencing neurological problems and had serious medical conditions. I was now at a facility where I participated in rehabilitation, including physical therapy while the doctors continued to monitor and evaluate me with the neurology team.

The strength in my left hand was still weak, but I felt hopeful and with time and physical therapy I believed I would regain my strength and be stronger. I pictured my strong left hand like before. Within the coming weeks I met with the occupational therapist, psychologist, vocational therapist, and physical therapist.

I was taught how to use a special flat board to transfer from my bed to the manual wheelchair. Sometimes the nurses used a special metal lift that they referred to as a "hoist" to transfer me off the bed to the manual wheelchair. This unusual device was tall with hydraulics and long metal cylinders that was made strong enough to lift a person with this strong metal device that did all the work so the nurses didn't have to lift me. This hoist would clamp and secure me like a swing, and then transported me in the air. It was interesting to me to know that there were inventions to carry people in the air without having to use a person's strength. The nurse would simply secure me inside while the metal machine did all the work. I would be hanging and transported like a stork that brought babies to their mothers wrapped in the big white diapers like I saw in cartoons in earlier years. I felt like I was a big baby being delivered by a stork, except in reality, I was being placed on my wheelchair or taken directly to the metal tub where I was placed to bathe.

The occupational therapist provided me with a reacher device that was similar to a stick with a grasp or clamp at the end. This device assisted me with lifting items easily from the floor or far away without much use of my body. For example, it reached for my socks or my blouse that were in a bag below and supported my ability to grab items that were on my shelf around me that were high or low. This device was very helpful and allowed me to easily grab items with little force from my hands, and I didn't have to bend my legs and risk falling or lose my balance. *What a great invention,* I thought. *Whoever invented this reacher appliance was a genius.*

I participated in the weekly support group meetings that were offered in English by a nice Caucasian social worker. On one of the days that I was being lifted from my bed with the hoist device, I asked one of the ladies who shared the room with me, *"¿Porque no vas al grupo de apoyo?"* (Why aren't you attending the weekly support group meetings?) Her response in Spanish was because the meetings are only in English and she doesn't understand what they are talking about. I asked the nurses and the social worker if they offered support group meetings in Spanish and the response was, "Unfortunately, we only have support group meetings in English due to budget cuts." I asked if it would be okay if I could translate the support group meeting discussions in Spanish so that the other woman in my room and the other patients that I met from other rooms down the hall who only spoke Spanish could also attend. I knew that the Spanish-speaking patients were not participating in these weekly support group meetings because everyone spoke English. They would, however, gather in their rooms or often visited me in my room to learn about what we had talked about in the meetings.

I continued to tell the counselor and the nurses that I spoke more English than Spanish but felt comfortable enough to translate or interpret the meetings to accommodate the Spanish-speaking patients. The nurse looked back at me with a perplexed look and in an initial tone of discontentment, said, "Great, now I have more patients to lift out of bed." From reading her body language and her tone I knew she was not too happy about this news at first. Soon thereafter, I could tell that she was simply being honest, and it reminded me of their complaints of being understaffed. I understood where she was coming from.

When I informed the Spanish-speaking patients that I would translate for them they were very interested in the news and began to ask questions about what we did at the group meeting. I replied, "We just share what we are going through and why we are here." I added,

"You don't have to say anything if you don't want to, just come." Even the English-speaking patients in my room now expressed a desire to get out of their beds and give the support group a try.

As I participated in the meetings and translated for the social worker that hosted these meetings I learned that many folks were feeling exactly like me. Similar sentiments were expressed related to the despair and confusion about what was going on with their body. It was obvious that we all had many emotions locked up inside that caused us to cry, yell, or simply shut down in disbelief. The participants reminisced about how their life was before the incident or accident. Some tearfully expressed what had happened to them that impacted not only their life but also that of their family members. Many expressed in the group that the caregiver or their partner who were not injured or disabled had a more difficult time than themselves recovering at the hospital.

It was reaffirming to me that many were in this position of helplessness and uncertainty. Besides the patients in the hospital, the families shared many of the same psychological implications. Every single aspect of who we were and what we did before was changed in an instant. It was almost like there was a sense of clarity that comes to you, recalling all the things you did before getting to this new low point in life and wishing you could go back there—wishing for something different to avoid what caused the NOW. The now, in my case, was not sure of what was happening to my body and brain, feeling out of control, weakness in my legs, paralysis or a shutdown of my lower extremities, abnormalities in my brain scans, spinal cord, dysfunction of my bladder and bowel movements, tingling sensations, and feelings of numbness in my body. All of that accompanied by the painful spasms that seemed to travel all over my body, my legs, my arms, my back, and especially on my head...and still not knowing why all this was happening was the worst feeling ever. Not knowing if I would die from this and wondering about my children's future made me very sad. I tried to make others feel better, but deep down, I was scared just like them.

Somehow, I was able to connect with the many different patients that lived with me now at this rehabilitation center. I was interested in them, and maybe they felt it. We spent many hours together, ate together, went to physical therapy together, and hung out in our rooms together and shared in long and deep conversations until late at night. We listened to music and shared snacks as well.

What I learned in this process was that our human natural instinct to stay connected seemed to increase when we were out of our comfort zone, especially when our family and those close to us were absent. Prior to being at this hospital, I used to be caught up in barely having enough time to spend with those in my circle of family and friends. I didn't pay as much attention to others in my community. I was consumed in my own conversations with those I knew, and especially when I was with close family and friends that I hadn't seen in a while. It wasn't that I wanted to be antisocial, rude, or disconnected from those around me that were not in my immediate circle. On the contrary, I liked being around others, but with so much going on in my own personal life with being a wife, mother, and daughter, I felt that I never seemed to have enough time to even connect with my family and close friends. Therefore, when we regrouped, it was our time to catch up. I did not notice or pay attention to my surroundings, and especially the dynamics of people living with disabilities around me. I am sure several wheeled past me as I think back, just like I am wheeling past others now.

I could choose to stay quiet and shut down in my new surroundings. It was an option that I tried at first but saw that people all around me were trying to do the same and somehow this sadness and despair united us with unspoken words. The feelings of uncertainty and despair were the unspoken emotions that hung silently in the air by many of the patients. My human and natural instinct to belong overcame my desire to shut down. We all had something in common and for whatever our reasons, we shared space and knew that we would be here for a while. My projected discharge date that I was told would be 6 months from when I arrived. For some it was closer to a year.

I met so many nice people residing in the 700 building neurology unit. Many had issues, lashing out in fear and frustration as they had a new reality check of how their identity had been changed. So many painful and heartfelt testimonies were shared in the now bilingual support groups that I was able to translate to the Spanish-speaking patients who were now a part of this weekly group. We may not have the same diagnosis, illness, or medical condition, however, we had the same longing to be heard. We were joined together and felt a part of something. The underlying reason for why we gathered was simply understood without explanation.

My husband and my young daughters came to visit me for a few hours every day, and during the weekends they stayed for longer periods. My roommates looked forward to their visits. Some felt like they knew my family too because I shared insights with them, and every time they came, they learned a little bit more about us as a family. My sisters brought snacks and items for me to share with them and even brought special requested goodies that a few would ask for as my sisters began to befriend them, becoming their visitors as well.

Initially, it was an adjustment for my daughters and husband to visit me at the rehabilitation center. My girls simply wanted me to go home with them and their daddy. They wanted us to play at home in our backyard so that we could go inside our house after playtime and they could cuddle with Mama. Oftentimes they cried when it was time for them to leave. I always tried my best to leave them with a funny story and brought laughter to them while they played in the nearby grassy park area that was made especially for patients to have an outdoor space for picnics, a barbeque, or a space away from the patient's room. I looked forward to when they came, and I got myself ready in my regular clothing. I didn't like to be seen in the hospital clothing. My girls played with their cousins, aunts, or with each other in the grassy area as Juan and I watched nearby. How I wanted to run and chase them and play like before. We made this time the happiest time of the day, and they were too busy having fun that they forgot where we were until it was time for them to leave. Priceless moments. As soon as they got ready to leave, sadness clouded their eyes and heavy spirits would fill the air. Their beautiful big brown eyes told me about their confusion and sadness. Some days they appeared fully adjusted. They became accustomed to seeing many people with different medical conditions who filled the long hospital hallways and the grassy area where they played.

As another month passed I learned even more about who my roommates were. One by one, I learned about their private and personal experiences that led to why and how they became a patient at the rehabilitation hospital. I also learned about their life before their illness or accident. These patients, or acquaintances, as I referred to them during the first week, had now become closer to me than many friendships that I had throughout my life. For me, these were my new friends that were now very much a part of my daily life. What I experienced with them was so different than any friendship I ever experienced. Maybe it was because we lived together in close quarters, all going through an incident or trauma that joined us by the neurologist and nurses. My friends outside from this place "back home" did not live with me as those that I was surrounded by here. My friends back home were people that I knew from years of going to school and working together. The circumstances at this rehabilitation hospital formed bonds that were deep, unique, and could not compare to the relationships that I had before being a patient.

Some of my new friends that lived in the neurology unit looked threatening. Some had large tattoos that began on their baldheads, faces, neck, and on many areas of their bodies displaying their names and sometimes their gang affiliations. There were unspoken messages that represented death of family or strangers. Some had painted murals like a map of history in colorful tattoo ink or in the blue ink that filled their body space. I learned that some of the names or symbols on their arms or legs signified family members who had passed away or represented the people and places they admired. Some had reasons for me to feel frightened, especially when they shared their gang affiliation. However, I was not a threat to them, seeing their scars and spinal cord injuries that resulted in their use of a wheelchair or had limited their mobility. Their inner spirit had softened despite the outward appearances. Their disability or paralysis gave them a new outlook regarding their current life.

There was a sense of vulnerability and desperation in the eyes of some of those I shared space with throughout this huge facility where we all crossed paths or gathered in the hallways, outside, and in places where we were free to roll around in. I sensed many were reaching out desperately for someone to take notice and longed for someone to have a conversation with them. They didn't scare me. I was immediately accepted. Maybe it was because I was also utilizing a wheelchair, or because I was a female and was approachable. Maybe it wasn't about them at all; maybe it was because I accepted them and the feeling was mutual. I also wanted to be connected to them.

I now think back of how different the relationships built under these circumstances would have been if I met them as they passed me down the street while I rushed about, quickly passing them wearing my high heels 4 or 5 months earlier. This facility reminded me of the *cholos,* or gang members, that lived alongside me in Lincoln Heights in my early years growing up with my sisters and mom. I also didn't fear the gang members, or *cholos,* that were in my neighborhood growing up, and I didn't see them as a threat. However, my mom discouraged me from getting too close to them for fear of me or my family getting in trouble.

I thought of a boy named Joey who was affiliated with a gang and walked me to school, and, yes, kissed me too. He was my first schoolboy crush in junior high school. When I had graduated from high school I learned that Joey's younger brother was shot and now lived with paralysis and brain injury. His mom tearfully shared this tragedy when I ran into her at the local market years ago and said her son was now like a vegetable. How easy my life path could have been changed based on my experiences and choices.

My grade school friend and neighbor Raul, a gang member and in my classroom, was shot and killed when he was 14. I didn't think of Raul as a gang member. I saw him as someone who was the same age as me, a funny and shy neighbor who shared classes with me throughout the years. We grew up together and lived in the same neighborhood.

My mom was our protector. At that time I didn't think of her as one; in fact, at times, I was resentful because she always kept us busy working, cleaning, and involved in activities. I felt this way toward her because she would always stop me from hanging out with Raul and his *cholo* friends.

My childhood activities included ballet folkloric, where we learned about our Mexican culture and danced to Spanish-language traditional music from many regions of Mexico. As a group of children well into our teen years, we practiced choreography and new routines most days during the week at the church recreation center we called *Busca*, especially during the summer months. My sister Jackie and I performed ballet folkloric for the general public with our dance group on some weekends. Once or twice we even performed on a TV show called *Angie's Garage*. A memorable performance was when we danced in Palm Springs with a celebrated Mexican musical group that provided live entertainment after our performance. We got to meet these aspiring group members and the ballet folkloric group stayed for the dance afterward.

When I reached the age of 14 I was accepted into the summer youth program that was made available to anyone who wished to participate from my neighborhood. My role was to assist the youth managers with community activities. Sometimes I assisted the nuns from Assumption Church in the weekly outreaches in the neighborhood. We would walk door to door to homes in Boyle Heights and City Terrace. The nuns, or "sisters," would instruct me to share messages that they wanted me to translate for them in Spanish as we met with families outside their homes. I proudly walked the streets with the "sisters" and was delighted to see that some of the children we went to visit in their homes did show up the next day for the free lunch program and participated in the arts and crafts activities that were offered at the church.

During that summer, the youth program also took us to field trips. We traveled on yellow school buses to various beaches and also took a trip to Catalina Island. The ride on a ship made me nauseated. However, once arriving on the island, we got over the seasick feeling because there was so much to see and enjoy on the day field trip.

This was our first time at such a beautiful island that seemed so far away. It seemed exclusive and felt like it was a secret place where only those who were wealthy could enjoy. The trip to Catalina Island seemed like it was only a few hours away from home. What a wonderful experience that I will remember, and a place where I hope to return to. We left the island filled with excitement, sticky from sweat, burned from the sun, and exhausted because we rode bikes and visited so many places during the half-day journey to an enchanted faraway island not so far from home.

Being a patient at the rehabilitation center triggered many experiences from my past as just shared. I was now paying attention to my surroundings and took the time to process and think of where I've been and to contemplate where I go from here. I questioned why it took me so long to take a break and see where I have been prior to being a patient at this facility. I realized that if we allow ourselves to travel deep into our past we can discover a great deal, and sometimes it is best to keep it far away so that we don't remember painful or uncomfortable feelings.

Our mind is interesting. Our brain is powerful enough to store and take us to moments we completely forgot about. I was struggling to be brave and honest with many feelings that were resurfacing. It was easier to share about growing up and only the fun time memories from my past then talking about the present, being at the hospital.

I see connections and parts of my past that have helped me along the way and also for years to come. For example, my mom was always trying to protect me and keep me safe. She wanted the best for me by keeping me busy in activities that have now become cherished memories.

The rehabilitation center represented a diversity of cultures, especially Latino and black. The young/old men/women were living with paralysis due to accidents or a medical diagnosis that changed their lives forever. Some had hope of a full recovery, but most had permanent paralysis. I wonder what has become of them now. For that brief period, we leaned on each other and needed each other. Now they were a tiny part of my past, but they made a big impact that changed me. I woke up to see that our lives could change at any moment...for the better or for the worse.

"Pay attention to your surroundings while also paying attention to you; make adjustments for happiness as life happens quickly." Simply Love

Chapter 5

My Shocking News

*P*articipating in the physical therapy at the rehabilitation center every week gave me hope that with time I would be able to walk again. I was now able to stand for 2 minutes at a time, with assistance, during an hour span. The dizziness and losing my balance while I attempted to walk continued, but for shorter durations.

After 2 months at the rehabilitation hospital I was able to stand with supportive leg devices, "braces," and with the assistance of the physical therapist. On this particular day, I was in the hallway with the physical therapist and her assistant. The physical therapist was holding me up with white bed sheets wrapped around my waist, and she was positioned behind me holding back the sheets that were tight on my waist. She helped me to take my first steps standing. I was holding on to the handrail with my left hand and my right hand and the right side of my body was supported by the nice male assistant while the physical therapist was standing behind me. Her body was leaning back while she held on to the white sheets that were tugging at my waist. The three of us were taking small steps together.

I felt faint, dizzy, and my entire body was hot. I was sweating but felt excited because I was not lying in my bed. I was standing with leg braces that went all the way up to my thighs. Together, we were in the process of taking a few steps at a time to walk even if it included the physical therapist and her assistant's support. It felt good to be out of my bedroom and not sitting in the wheelchair.

I was taking my first steps and conversing with the physical therapist when I saw the neurologist resident that had been attending me at this facility. He was walking quickly toward me and gave me a half smile and said to me in passing, "Oh, by the way, we know what is wrong with you. You have been diagnosed with multiple sclerosis, and you will probably never walk again." I played back his words in my head, and my body began to feel weak. My legs were shaking and so were my hands. I wanted him to tell me again what he said because I didn't think that I heard correctly. When I looked up, he was already turning the hallway. He was gone, and I could no longer see him.

I felt an urge to sit down. My wheelchair was close by, so I sat. I sat in silence. I felt the warm tears that began to run by the side of my face. My heart was beating fast. I asked the physical therapist to please take me to my bed. We were quiet as she assisted me back onto my bed and assisted me with taking off my heavy leg braces. I asked her to please close my drapes that surrounded my bed. As soon as the drapes closed completely, I began to shake more, to sweat profusely, and felt an ache in my stomach. My silent cries turned to a loud painful scream. Many thoughts began to enter my mind.

The first thought that came to my mind was, *Oh my God, I'm going to die.* I began to think about my nice neighbor Mrs. Margo who had the diagnosis of MS and who used to live right across the street from my family and me. Our home faced where Mrs. Margo used to live. Her husband cared for her, and he would tell us about how his wife used to enjoy life with him and his two daughters. I witnessed her health deteriorate. I pictured her as she used to sit in her wheelchair despondent most days before being transferred to a nursing home. I rarely saw Mrs. Margo because she used to stay indoors most of the time and when we would go over to speak with her she often appeared confused, disoriented, and her speech was slurred which made it difficult for us to understand her. But her composure and her eyes welcomed us, and she was friendly.

In later years, it was noticeable that Mrs. Margo's illness had deteriorated quite a bit. She now appeared frustrated and uncomfortable, as her pain was evident, and even with these complications she made attempts to communicate with us, reminding me that she was a nice neighbor. Their home was filled with photos of Mrs. Margo during a period when she was younger, vibrant, and without MS. The photos were taken alongside her two young daughters.

I recalled one specific day when Mrs. Margo's daughter came to say hello to me while I was getting groceries from my car. She sadly expressed that she had just came back from visiting her mom at the nursing home and that she was excited to tell her mom that she would be getting married. However, her facial expressions changed to sadness as she put her head down and shared that her mother did not recognize her as she stood before her mommy in her wedding gown. I recalled how I hugged Patricia, the daughter, as I was speechless and didn't know what to say. I felt sad and stayed quiet as she rushed back into the house where her mother used to live across the street from us to see her dad.

Mrs. Margo passed away from MS complications and my family and I went to her funeral. It was horrible to witness the pain when her husband Federico and daughters lost their mom to MS. This was all that I knew about multiple sclerosis.

In my private thoughts while I lay in bed near my roommates at the rehabilitation center I began to think about all I had remembered about Mrs. Margo and my stomach ached. I did not want to die like she did from progressive MS complications. I wanted to see my daughters Jacqueline and Johnnie grow up. I needed to see my girls now. I kept telling myself, "I want to go home and take care of my girls. No one will love my girls like I do." I didn't want them to see me deteriorate with MS. I want to tell them that Mommy will be home soon and that Mama would be driving them to the zoo. I wanted to run out of this place and drive to my family, but I knew that my legs were weak, my balance was off, and I was afraid to fall again. Now on this day I was told that I might *never* walk again, and, yes, I knew firsthand what MS could do. I witnessed it with Mrs. Margo who lived right across from me. I thought to myself, *I don't want my speech to become slurred or my mind to become confused, disoriented, or worse, lose my memory. No, I don't want this MS to take away my voice that sings happy and funny songs that I composed that share lessons about life and positive loving thoughts.* These songs were silly and made my girls laugh and sing along. I have more songs in my head that I still haven't shared that are funny and rhyme about bubble gum and fun in the sun. I wanted to go outside and splash in puddles in the rain with Johnnie and Jackie like we did before. I wanted to dance with my girls near the worms that we only saw when it rained hard while our neighbors rushed to go inside.

When I reflected on how Mrs. Margo became confused and forgot who her daughter was, I painfully moaned and couldn't seem to get ahold of myself. I had so much that I still wanted to teach my girls and show them. My cries became uncontrollable and exhausting.

The evening nurse tried to calm me down by telling me that everything would be okay. However, despite her heartfelt concern, her words didn't seem to make me feel better. I asked her to please call my husband. I needed to see my husband. I yelled out once more, "Please call my husband." I was given a sedative and cried myself to sleep.

That same evening my husband's gentle kiss on my lips awakened me in the dark. It was nighttime now, and the lights were turned off in our room. We held each other as I told him, "I have MS, the same illness that Mrs. Margo had, and now she is dead." I told Juan, "I am scared. I don't want to die. I don't want to die, and I want to raise our daughters with you and go home with you tonight." It was all I could think of saying and wanted to do. His eyes told me he was as scared as I was. He held me for a long time. I told him I was sorry to put him through this, and we cried quietly. It was after visiting hours. I was thankful that the nurse had contacted Juan, and that he was there with me.

My roommates were in their beds resting beside me in the dark. I knew that they were listening, and I also knew that they shared my sadness quietly while they lay near me a few feet away.

Juan's last words to me before he left were, "Don't worry, you will be okay. I love you. Sleep now." We kissed good night, and he left to go to my mom's house where the girls were staying. Morning soon came. I did not feel like eating or bathing or having visitors either. I did not like the way I felt, but this was how I felt. I missed the support group meeting that was held down the hall again.

In the coming week, I finally began to feel better. I asked one of the nurses if she had any information about MS so that I could learn more. She checked and said they did not have any brochures about it, but that she would look around and see what she could find. She came back several days later carrying a big old medical book. I found the definition quickly and learned that it was a neurological disorder that affected the brain, central nervous system, and spinal cord. The short article said that there were no cure or treatment options, other than medicine for pain and spasms. It showed a person with progressive MS, naked, and the person looked almost like a skeleton in a fetal position in pain. It didn't explain clearly how a person contracted MS. Limited information left it open for me to interpret that it could be hereditary or environmental. The brief information left me with wanting to learn more.

Other literature showcased studies conducted among the American population and referred to MS as a disease or disorder that affected Caucasian Americans. Please keep in mind that the year that I was diagnosed with MS was in the summer of 1990. During this time, the Internet communication like we use today was nonexistent. In fact, e-mailing and knowledge of the Internet and texting was not available yet. The Internet usage became available mid-1995. Therefore, the main form of communication of news back then when I was diagnosed was by calling someone on the telephone, or possibly reading materials in English only from the library textbooks that were often outdated or scarcely available.

A week had passed since I had received the diagnosis of multiple sclerosis by the neurology resident. As I lay in my bed recalling how he had shared this news with me, I became sad, then angry because I felt that the manner that he had shared this news was insensitive and not appropriate. I pictured him again rushing past me without giving me a moment to ask a question or process what he had just said. This was not acceptable. At first I discounted my feelings by saying that the resident doctor was probably so busy with seeing so many patients. He was a doctor, after all, and must have so much on his mind, and naturally, he didn't realize how this news that he just blurted out to me in passing quickly in the hallway would affect me. Then I thought again and said to myself, no, I would not want anyone else to be given life-changing news in the manner that I was told, quickly and in the hallway, without a second to stop for me to ask a question. *"We know what is wrong with you. You have been diagnosed with multiple sclerosis, and you will probably never walk again."* This was an awful way for a doctor to communicate with his patient as he rushed quickly down the hallway without a second thought.

In the coming days, as I continued to process this terrible news, I thought of how I would have preferred hearing it. Maybe it was because I was sad or mad about the news that I felt compelled to let the neurologist resident's superior (boss) know of the manner that I was told. It became my priority to inform the chief neurologist of this incident. Of course, it wouldn't change the fact that now I have the diagnosis of MS. But I felt strongly that I wanted to make sure that others given news of a diagnosis of a devastating illness should not be told like it was said to me. Was I just so upset that I just wanted to lash out at someone and the first person to get mad at was the doctor that gave me the news? Maybe, but I still felt that for future patients getting news from this doctor or others who might say it in a similar way should know that there are other ways or more sensitive approaches to communicate with patients. For example, maybe if I had received this news in a conference room with my husband and possibly my mom and sisters who could have given me the support that I felt I needed. I would have preferred hearing this news in a private setting, and especially with my husband. I would have appreciated learning about what this condition meant. I would have wanted to know what steps I must take to prepare for my future. Furthermore, how about support for the family members and children? I felt strongly that his approach was not very sensitive or appropriate.

I requested to see the chief of neurology to discuss my discontentment with how I was given my diagnosis. She came to see me on the same day that I requested to speak with her. She agreed that this was not the best way to give someone a diagnosis. I thanked her for coming to see me, and I expressed in a calm but serious manner that it was important for me that she reinforces to the medical team, especially the physicians, the importance of taking time out to talk with patients about giving them sad or bad news. She apologized for him. I responded that I was not asking for her apology. I shared I simply wanted her to know how devastated I was when I was given the news by the resident in the hallway, and that I did not want others to get news like I did in that same manner.

That afternoon the resident that rushed away after giving me my diagnosis came to see me and apologized for how he delivered the information. I accepted his apology and echoed the sentiment that I had shared earlier that morning with the chief of neurology.

When my eldest sister Debbie would visit me, she exercised my legs from my bed. Debbie would say that I needed to keep moving my legs, and that I had to do more leg exercises. She brought lotions and rubbed them on my legs. She helped to make me feel better; she took turns to bring my daughters to visit when my husband and sister Jackie were at work. She brought me favorite deviled egg sandwiches that she prepared on white bread for many of us to enjoy.

My young nephew who was 6 years old at the time would refer to me as "Nina Robocop" as he observed me taking steps at the courtyard with the physical therapist. He would yell out with excitement and in his deep voice say, "Nina Robocop" as I practiced walking in the courtyard ramp that had handrails where I did physical therapy outside by the big trees in the shade. My leg braces that went up to my thighs securely wrapped and reinforced my legs to stand strong were modified for me and made me feel safe while I took my steps on the ramp. Wearing the steel metal arm braces and practicing walking was my sign that I would walk again. It was confusing and frustrating when I used the arm braces because my brain would sometimes want to go one way and the arm braces didn't go in the direction they were supposed to. Sometimes my legs in braces also wanted to go at a different pace and direction.

For a few moments at a time I practiced with the assistance of the physical therapist. Sometimes the walking made me dizzy and my right foot would drop, causing me to trip and fall forward. I was only able to stand for a few minutes at a time before needing to rest my legs that weakened and sometimes felt numb. It was frustrating to see that when I would put my left foot forward, it took time for it to take a step and the right leg would not follow in balance. It was like my brain was taking its time to communicate with my body.

I had to use a catheter because I had no control of my bladder and my left hand still didn't grab as strong as my right hand did. I had another MRI and tests done to monitor my progress. Psychological assessment was also conducted to evaluate my mood and to determine if I was depressed. I followed up with a psychologist who assisted me with understanding this new way of living. We discussed the importance of communicating our feelings with those that we trusted, and naturally, I thought of my family.

One late afternoon my neurologist came to tell me that I would need to stay in the hospital for a total of 6 months to continue with my physical therapy and ongoing appointments and treatments with the different departments. I pleaded with my neurologist and shared that I needed to go home and be with my husband and my family. I insisted that home was where I would improve my physical therapy. I needed to sleep on my own bed, with my husband next to me. I missed having my daughters close to me. How I miss their smell and hearing their voices and me responding to their many random questions that were innocent, straightforward, and filled with curiosity. I smiled as I thought of Johnnie's first words to me the night before, "Look, Mama (speaking rather fast), I brought a brush to comb your hair, and then we go home okay, Mama?"

Jacqueline, on the other hand, told me one more time, "Just come home, Mama, it smells bad in this room; home smells better," as if to think that because I agreed with her and said yes, it did have an unusual smell and was different from home. She was right, of course. It smelled better at home and for her, that was a good enough reason to go home. She kept repeating to me in her deep, serious tone, "Come on, Mama, let's go home now. Why you have to stay here?" Her repeated question was echoed again. "Mama, why it smells here? I don't like the way it smells here. Come home now so you can sleep on your real bed with Daddy." Her words were innocent and honest. I could feel that she meant every word and looked confused as I said once more, "Mama will need to stay here with the nurses and doctors so that I can get better soon." I would smile and respond, "Yes, someday soon, Mama will be home in our comfy home that smells delicious!" I would squeeze my girls tight and make them laugh right before it was time again to say good night and watch them leave my room in slow motion and curious about my other roommates who observed them and also waved good-bye.

Finally, a conference meeting was scheduled with my family for the following week so that the medical team and my family could discuss and evaluate my request to be discharged 3 months earlier than recommended by the medical team. The conference meeting went well, and my family came and supported my request to go home earlier. My family was able to demonstrate to the medical team that I had a supportive family and that it would be in my best interest and that of our small children that I be discharged early and go home. I agreed to continue to come back to the rehabilitation outpatient clinic for my weekly physical therapy appointments and continue with other ongoing appointments that were scheduled with various departments, including the neurology MS outpatient clinic, physical therapy, orthopedic specialist, ophthalmologist, occupational therapy, and continue to be in touch with the psychologist.

My family and I were so pleased that our request to leave 3 months earlier was granted, and we were so excited that in the following week I would be transitioning for discharge and going home soon.

As I prepared for my discharge, I experienced many emotions. I felt happy but didn't want my roommates to know how happy I was, because I also felt their sadness as they wished that they could also leave. We all knew that once we were discharged, we would continue with our separate lives and possibly not see each other ever again. We would joke among ourselves and say to each other, "Whoever leaves this place first, don't worry about coming back to visit, because if you are feeling like me, once discharged, returning back here would be the *last* place you want to go." No hard feelings, it was just the way it was and what we all said jokingly. Now, it didn't feel funny. No one was laughing. So this was kind of my roommates and I saying, "It's okay if you don't come back to see me." I felt sad leaving them because we had grown to know each other, an experience like no other, living with a group of ladies who were scared like me, uncertain of their future, and trying their best to be hopeful and kind.

Some of the patients I met during my stay had families to go home to, while others expressed that they had no one to care about them. Ms. Lori, a young victim of multiple gunshot wounds in her early twenties, was told that she wouldn't be discharged anytime soon. She also knew that from this place she would be transferring to a senior nursing center where she would live to obtain needed health care on a daily basis due to the severity of her medical condition that would require her to have nurses on a daily basis. However, she would not be leaving anytime soon. That was what her doctor told her. She still had one more surgery to undergo. I thought to myself, not the best place for a young lady in her twenties. Unfortunately, there were no other facilities available for her age group. What hope would she have there, I thought to myself. For now, her care at the rehabilitation hospital was anticipated to continue for another 5 months.

Ms. Lori made me think that her condition could worsen simply because she would possibly see many elderly patients die. She would witness their suffering while they were in the last phase of their life. I knew that this reality made me feel depressed and less hopeful for her. I quietly felt grateful that I had a family to go home to and that my care did not require for me to be transferring to a nursing home after being discharged. However, it made me think of many others who I had met and would be leaving in the same situation as Ms. Lori, and that situation did not sit well with me. I will miss Ms. Lori's positive energy and funny private jokes that we shared.

I tried not to be close to my roommates—that is what I kept telling myself as I prepared to leave this place that was my home for approximately 3 months. I didn't want to miss them, but how can I not miss this beautiful special woman who shared with me many nights of cries, laughs, and especially conversations that spoke of deep secrets or of challenges that we shared. We hugged, said farewell, and we all knew that we would probably never see each other again . . .

"Connections and special moments transpire when you let go of biases and pride and invite others in with an open heart." Simply Love

Chapter 6

Mobility Sparks a New Beginning

*M*y cheerful nurse smiled as she saw me observing my new manual wheelchair that had arrived and was ordered specifically for me to take home. The new wheelchair was now located on the side of my bed. She remarked, "Honey, your sparkling wheels are ready for you." I smiled as if to say, "Yes, I know." I thought to myself, this mobility sparks a new beginning, a new way of being, and I knew for a fact that my life that I had before this incident had forever changed. I was uncertain of my future, and I knew that many more changes were in motion and more would come.

I asked my nurse to assist and push me on my wheelchair while I sat on my comfy new wheels. She took me right outside my room door as I held on to one of my bags filled with my personal belongings. I was too excited and didn't want to be on my bed when Juan arrived to take me home. From the angle outside my room door, I could see down the long hallway as I waited in anticipation for Juan. My eyebrows were neatly plucked, my thick dark black hair was washed and combed, hanging straight down at my shoulders. I was no longer wearing the faded hospital gown that I used to sleep in. Instead, I was wearing a new colorful summer dress that my sister Jackie brought me a few days ago. The warm bath that I had earlier that morning was refreshing. It felt different because I knew that this day would be my last bath here. I would be going home early that afternoon. I could smell the lotion that my sister Debbie had brought for me that I slowly massaged onto my legs and body earlier that morning.

I reflected on when I used to dance ballet folkloric as a young girl and the fun times at the disco when I wore my high heels and danced until early hours in the mornings with my girlfriends Ofelia and Irma or with my sisters before meeting Juan. I was interrupted in my thoughts by one of the patients who passed near me quickly in his wheelchair. He said he was headed to his physical therapy appointment but wanted to make sure he said good-bye and wished me well before I left. A reminder of the many nice persons I had met that knew I was going home.

I adjusted my body and sat up straight in my wheelchair as I saw my reflection that showed me that I was slouched with my shoulders leaned forward. The brand-new wheelchair was comfortable and fit me perfectly. The metal chrome wheels were shiny too. I never noticed before how there were various types of wheelchairs and how they were made specifically for all body types, sizes, and needs. For instance, if someone had strong upper mobility, their wheelchair might be lighter and made in a way so that the person can easily lift or move swiftly with their hands. Other wheelchairs were made heavier or had handles for someone else to push if the person had limited upper mobility. Yet others had sophisticated electronics and hydraulics that took care of most of the movement with a simple tap for those individuals who needed more assistance.

I came out of my daydreaming when I saw Juan walking fast toward me. He was still at a distance away, but I recognized his walk, and as he got closer I felt my heart beat faster, and, yes, this was my Juan. I knew that he knew it was me that was staring at him from the faraway distance as he began to walk more quickly. His body told me that he was getting shy and embarrassed. He got shy when he knew that I was watching him, similar to when we used to date, like our first night at the disco dancing to Donna Summer.

As our eyes met he gave me a faint smile and was staring and trying not to stare, but he couldn't help himself. I could feel that he was excited to see me too. Soon he reached me and bent down to kiss my lips as I immediately reached up at the same time and pulled my arms upward to wrap them around his shoulders as tight as I could from my wheelchair. Juan seemed a bit nervous, or maybe anxious was a better word. I could tell that he wanted to take me away quickly. He rushed to gather my bags that he hung on each side of the wheelchair. I grabbed another white bag to hold on my lap that contained my mementos, the get-well cards and photos of my family that they had brought months ago, including the cards from the ICU from months prior. All of these items wrapped neatly in my white plastic bags reminded me of fun times experienced before my diagnosis of multiple sclerosis and that I was not the same person as before.

I smiled again as I thought of my family, friends, and neighbors that came to visit me at the hospital or sent flowers and cards these past months. The get-well cards that hung around my bed space helped me to remember that my stay was temporary and now they were traveling home with me, leaving behind an empty space for the next person who would share intimate moments with strangers who will be their family if they choose to let them in.

The photos of my family were the same people that I loved and missed; I felt that their love was the same. I was uncertain of how the new Irma would affect how they loved me or how I would love me.

Especially when I was feeling different, uncertain, and alone, even though I knew that I had a beautiful family to go home to. How selfish of me to have these thoughts when I was surrounded by many who loved me. How could these ugly feelings of sadness and despair be possible? I thought to myself, I was very confused.

Juan wheeled me toward the nurse's station as my nurse was already walking toward us to give us the discharge plan. She reviewed the multiple appointments that were already scheduled for me to return as an outpatient in the coming weeks and months, along with sharing other papers that were important to take with us as part of my discharge plan. The discharge nurse said her final good-bye after I had said my farewell to my roommates. We all shared tears as we expressed our mutual gratitude for the time together. Reality hit that I was really going home and that I was not the same person that I was 4 months ago.

I was forced to deal with changes that I could feel were happening inside my body that I didn't ask for. My thoughts were different. I used to preoccupy my thinking with what I would make for dinner. Would I clean the bathroom today and vacuum tomorrow? Instead, now, my thoughts were "I want to drive again," "I don't want to go outside in this wheelchair," or "how would my bladder dysfunction affect me when I left my house to go to the store?" I was forced to see that others would not see me the same either. I felt losses that I wasn't prepared for, the loss of my balance or strength to walk, the loss of my independence, the loss of who I used to be was gone. In a matter of seconds, my life changed... for possibly the worse. I didn't recognize this vulnerable "Irma" who was scared, weak, and out of control. I didn't have the same identity, I didn't know who I was anymore...I was wearing a diaper. Yes, they call it an "adult protective garment," but it was a diaper. A diaper similar to what my almost 3- and 4-year-old daughters stopped wearing when they were 11 months and 1 year old. Now they too may have to wear diapers again since they had a few accidents of wetting the bed since I left them.

The doctor told me that I might not feel any sensation down "there," you know, my private area, due to the weakness and lower extremities paralysis that may be permanent. My husband would want to be intimate with me. I wanted to be intimate with him too. I didn't want to find out that I might not have any sexual sensation down there. I told myself that I couldn't deal with finding this out right now; right now, I just had to get home to my girls and get better.

Juan shared that the girls were with my mom and stepdad, "Grandpa" to the girls, and that he would bring them home the following morning. I missed them but understood why he didn't bring them to pick me up. It was now late in the afternoon, and it was best that we spent time with each other to talk.

I felt like I was on our first date with him, and that I was someone else, a stranger. I felt nervous and strange, and he seemed weird and not himself. He was not making any sense as he talked fast, trying to tell me about his work and our friends that wanted to see me. Did Juan also change? I tried to listen, but my mind kept wandering as I looked out the window and noticed a woman pushing a stroller that had a child in it and grocery bags on the side of each handle. It made me smile to watch them cross the street in front of us at the stoplight. This brief moment reminded me of when I would take our girls to the Los Angeles Zoo in their strollers with my sister Debbie and my nephew. Sometimes other family members would accompany us since I had an annual zoo membership pass. It was fun to go to the zoo to witness my girls interact with their cousin and wildlife animals, trees, and bugs. We practically lived at the zoo. Every week was a different part of the zoo that we would visit and a weekly ritual that also included a homemade lunch and healthy snacks. I wanted to take them to the zoo again soon. I was glad to know that my girls were walking more with their strong little legs and that they rarely used a stroller anymore and preferred pushing it. I wanted to walk strong too. I didn't want to return to the zoo in a wheelchair.

My husband interrupted my thoughts and shared in a comforting tone that our neighbors and friends had called and that they had expressed wanting to come over tomorrow or during the weekend. I smiled but responded that I didn't want to see anyone tomorrow. Maybe the following weekend would be nice, but not now. I told him that I only wanted to be with our girls and him. I asked if he could please bring them home early tomorrow and that maybe I would go with him to pick them up. I thought about it some more and changed my mind and asked if he could please pick them up early. I didn't feel like visiting my parents just yet. My parents' home had several stairs and I didn't want to think of that situation yet. He agreed.

I kept telling myself that I had to get better soon because my girls needed me strong. I could not be sad. I could not show Juan what I was feeling inside. I secretly felt mad, and I would not allow myself to cry is what I kept telling myself. I quietly cried though on the way home. I quietly felt sad, then happy, that I would be home soon. Then I was very upset that I would not be able to walk up the stairs of our newly remodeled home that was now a two-story house. My hands began to sweat as we were less than 1 mile away from our home.

It was now early evening and it was beginning to get dark. I leaned forward in anticipation as I saw our home. I pictured myself running up the stairs. Juan drove a little bit faster and stopped quickly at our front gate. He backed the car in the driveway and helped me to transfer to the wheelchair and proceeded to take me in to our home from the back door entrance. We both realized that going inside from the front door would be more difficult given the step that was right before the door. We agreed that the front and the back door into the house were not accessible for the wheelchair and me. We decided that it would work best if we entered from the back door and from the laundry room into the kitchen.

I didn't want to see my neighbors and going in from the back door was best. Juan pushed my wheelchair up a small step that led into the laundry room and up another step that went straight into our kitchen. We both saw the step and Juan yelled out "hold on" while he pulled my wheelchair back and then forward so that he could push me into the kitchen. We began to laugh as my back landed hard in the wheelchair and now we were in our kitchen. As soon as Juan turned on the kitchen lights I immediately noticed the new white tile that had just been installed on the floor. *Wow!* It looked beautiful and sparkling clean. The grout that was supposed to be in between the tiles was not finished or fully installed yet. Therefore, as Juan began to push me in the kitchen, I began to crack some of the tiles as he pushed me in my wheelchair. Juan said, "It's okay, baby, we haven't finished putting in the grout yet; that's why it cracked. I will fill it in tomorrow, don't worry. I have extra tile in the garage."

As he went back outside to bring in the bags and items from the car, I rolled myself in front of the oven. Two ovens were stacked above each other; the top part was the oven and the bottom part was the oven broiler. I noticed my reflection on the oven's clear glass and saw my shadow reflection that was me at eye level sitting in my wheelchair. I wiped my tears quickly as I heard Juan coming. He was so excited to show me our master bathroom that was upstairs. Juan carried me in his arms up the stairs. He was proud to show me all the work he had been doing while I was away. The gray carpet that began in the living room and up the stairs smelled like new clean carpet. Yes, this was the color that I picked out from the carpet samples that he had brought me months ago at the hospital. How perfect it was mounted in each corner.

As we made it upstairs and entered the master bedroom, immediately to my left was the fireplace. The fireplace was stunning with the dark gray and black lines that looked like strands of thin branches within the tile that surrounded the fireplace and blended perfectly with the gray carpet that filled our new master bedroom. The high ceilings and large bay windows located at each side of the walls were breathtaking. Our upstairs new home was absolutely amazing. The highlight for me was when he turned on the lights in the master bathroom that displayed the black-and-white tile and step into the black Jacuzzi tub that was big enough for the two of us. It reminded me of a piano outline, a long circular step that circled around the beautiful Jacuzzi tub. Above the Jacuzzi was a ceiling window that showed the outside clouds and to my left side was the large bay window that displayed our backyard. A private bathroom located on one side had a telephone installed on the wall and on the opposite side was the shower with two seats inside. Immediately before entering the clear glass shower was another phone that was mounted outside of the shower wall. So much thoughtful detail and design made especially for us.

I remembered the day that Juan brought me those different colored samples of carpet while I was at the hospital. He had asked me to choose the color and also brought tile samples. How uninterested I was to pick out a carpet or tile for our now two-story home. It seemed so long ago, and I did not care about this important detail. Now, on this day, I was so happy that he went with the soft gray carpet that I had liked among the other sample colors that he had brought me. Juan knew what I liked. Even though when he had originally asked me to pick it while I was at the ICU I had told him "put whatever color you like, I don't care, what does it matter? I can't walk upstairs anymore." I was glad that he went with the color that I was drawn to. I barely remembered this color until I got closer and he turned on the dim light that he installed near my bed and more dim lights that were above the high ceiling and in various parts of the bedroom. This room set the tone for romance! I was so proud of Juan and so happy to see all that he had accomplished while I was away.

I forgot for a brief moment that we were now in an upstairs home. As much as I loved this new home, it was no longer practical. We knew that it would be difficult for me to walk up and down the stairs. My limited mobility and my need for assistance was a concern but neither of us said this out loud. Our excitement for what Juan accomplished kept our spirits happy and was what we focused on. I didn't bring up the challenges that were present now, and neither did he.

Juan wanted to carry me back downstairs. Instead, I said, "No, wait." I asked him to help me on to the floor by the upstairs guardrail. I sat at the top of the stairs and immediately, without telling him what I was about to do, I began to push myself down each stair by sitting on my butt and pushing myself down. Slowly on my butt, I bumped down each stair. I felt like a kid playing on the stairs. I laughed out loud. When I looked up at Juan he had a perplexed look on his face and didn't seem to see the humor in what I was doing. He watched in silence and finally met me downstairs when I made it to the bottom of the 14 steps to the living-room floor. Juan helped me back on the wheelchair that was at the side of the handrail near the bottom of the stairs. We realized that for now as much as I loved him carrying me up the stairs and carrying me down the stairs he shouldn't have to do this. He could hurt his back. I had my leg braces and arm braces downstairs. I would use them as much as I could and practice holding on to the staircase. I would build my strength once I felt my balance stronger. If only we knew ahead of time that I would need to use a wheelchair or that our life would be different we would have never added a second-story addition to our home. I thought of all the details Juan put into our now two-story home that he made especially for us. I would love it and embrace it the best I could and so what if we slept downstairs sometimes? That would be okay.

Juan and I did go back up that night and slept in our upstairs master bedroom. I watched him sleep. I could hear his breathing, my *mijo* Juan was exhausted, and it felt good to cuddle next to him in our new bed. I felt safe again. As night turned to early morning, I lay in bed mesmerized by the high ceiling and arched window that let the sun in. Everything around me looked more beautiful than it did the night before, and the details that Juan brought to our new two-story home was breathtaking.

That morning we quickly ate cereal in the kitchen and shared a sense of urgency to have our girls back home. I wheeled myself to watch him drive off near the living-room bay window since I decided to not go with him to pick up our girls from Gramma and Grampa's house. I was excited to know that soon I would have my girls back home with us. I hardly slept the night before just thinking about them and playing in my head what I planned to say and do with them when they arrived in a little while.

Over 4 months had passed quickly and yet, the experiences endured in this process had changed me forever. I felt and saw myself in an entirely different way. I grew up in many ways these past 4 months and had to face a new reality that had impacted many aspects of my life and that of others close to me.

Remembering Mrs. Margo and the painful progression that she experienced with her family that we witnessed on a daily basis, how ironic that her house was located right across the street from ours. I used to see her look out their front bay window while we played in the front yard with the girls. She used to enjoy watching us while Juan and I worked on the yard or when we talked in the driveway with her husband who always made an effort to bring snacks and goodies for the girls and gifts for the family. We would wave to her every time we noticed her at the window.

As I reminisced about the past I was reminded of my new reality as I touched my legs and I could feel that they were weak. It was like I still was in disbelief that so much had transpired. I had problems with my balance when I tried to stand from my wheelchair. From the outside I looked the same. I was wearing my favorite summer dress and comfy sandals while I was sitting in the brand-new black seat and shiny chrome wheelchair. I thought about how I may not have any sensation down "there," you know, my private part. I did not feel sexy anymore. I was afraid to find out if I would be able to feel Juan's touch. Then I reassured myself that I would because I felt excitement and my heart beat fast when my body touched his last night while we lay in bed cuddled and close. However, I wasn't sure and was not ready to be intimate yet; not now. Maybe he would not want me anymore, maybe it would be different and not the same—or worst, maybe he would not desire me anymore. I wouldn't blame him if he decided to leave me. I touched my dress near my private area and felt my diaper. I was not the same person.

I didn't want to think of this any longer. The thought of Juan leaving me or picturing him with someone else made me uncomfortable. I wanted to go back upstairs and look at the fireplace in our bedroom again and see the beautiful black and strands of gray tile that surrounded the fireplace. Juan had left already. I did not want to try to go upstairs while I was alone, not today. It would take too much work. I decided instead to remain downstairs by the living-room bay window that faced where Mrs. Margo used to live.

For a split second as I looked outside the bay window and from my wheelchair I asked myself, have I turned into her? It was just a few years ago that Mrs. Margo was sitting at her front bay window looking and observing us as we played and worked outside. This thought brought a sense of anxiety as I felt my heart beat faster. Therefore, I switched my thinking to the good feeling I got every time I looked at Juan and he would blush and talk fast, and the thought of my girls made me smile because they were coming home soon.

I felt pride and admiration for Juan because I knew how hard he had been working while I had been away. I drifted back to the gray carpet that was soft and the big white arch windows in our bedroom that allowed the light to enter and bring sunshine. I could barely hear the birds on the roof. How interesting that Juan had installed phone outlets by the entrance to the shower and by the toilet seat that was privately located in a room away from the shower and Jacuzzi tub. Juan had thought of everything, and how nice of him to have a customized octagon window placed perfectly in the upstairs hallway so that it was positioned at my eye level when standing. Juan had shared before that he positioned the octagon window just right for my height so that when I wanted to see the mountains that were sometimes covered in snow, all I had to do was stand in the hallway by the handrail and admire the beauty.

I was excited and so happy to be home. However, I was not ready to go outside. I did not want any visitors either. I just wanted to absorb my new home with my husband and daughters. I sat in silence and waited for Juan and our girls to come home. I could hear the birds chirping louder in the quiet house. I smiled with anticipation as I pictured my girls home and thought of the normal talking and talking that they did with each other and with us. They would have many more questions when they returned home. I could hardly wait to witness their sharing of innocent conversations.

"There is no place like home." Simply Amor

Chapter 7

Mijas' Smiles Make a Positive Difference

*M*ija is a Spanish expression to describe "daughter" and my young daughters had just arrived home to Mama! I saw the car pull up in the driveway and watched Juan walk quickly to close the gate. He looked excited as he hurried back to the car to unlock and open the backseat door. I could tell that he was helping them with unlocking their car seats.

Soon my *mijas* ran past the front porch with the biggest smiles on their faces. They stopped to look at me from the front porch bay window. They noticed me watching them and pressed their faces on the windowpane, smiled, and waved as they ran to the front door. My *mijas'* smiles made a positive difference and immediately improved my mood. Now with them in the home the air all around me felt soothing, like a breath of fresh air. Both girls were carrying their special blankets that I gave them since birth. This special first blanket had been washed many, many times. The blankets were faded and had been patched up numerous times throughout the years. You can imagine how many places their special blanket has traveled. Jacqueline ran inside ahead of her sister carrying tightly her white Little Mommy bear that was wrapped inside her blanket.

My mom had a routine of putting on a uniquely scented lotion after her bath. A ritual that now she shared with her granddaughters. I could smell the special lotion that was the only lotion scent that their grandma liked. Now Grandma's scent was on them as I held them close in my arms.

Johnnie and Jackie's ponytails were slicked back nice and neat. Both girls were talking at once, giving me updates of what they did at Gramma and Grampa's house.

They immediately began to check out their mama's wheelchair. Jacqueline wanted to know if they could sit on my lap. Johnnie immediately said, "No, sistha, don't hurt Mama's legs" and asked if she could push me. Jacqueline began to crawl up to sit on my lap ignoring her sister's comment and said, "Daddy and sister could push us outside." Before I could even respond, Johnnie went to open the front door as wide as she could. I did not plan to go outside today. But they were persistent and Johnnie wanted to push me now. Finally I agreed, and we all went outside, despite it not being what I wanted to do right then. Jacqueline sat on my lap while her sister pushed me with the assistance of her dad.

Before I knew it, we were strolling out of the driveway and down the street. My *mijitas* said they wanted to show Josie, Martha, Vicki, Lupe, Alfredo, Tony, Frank, etc., and all our other friends and neighbors that lived in our cul-de-sac, that Mama was home. Our friends began to watch us from a distance and slowly they began to gather and walk toward us as we strolled further away toward the main street. Before I knew it, we reunited with our neighbors who had many great messages and dialogues with the girls. Frank began to comment about how tall they were getting and multiple voices talking at once expressing in English and Spanish how excited they were that I was back home. My neighbors offered support and wanted me to know that they were here for us.

I invited our neighbors to follow us back to the house for coffee or tea. Yes, here I was inviting them to come over even though I had said moments before that I didn't want to see anyone. Once I saw my neighbors it was easy to want to spend time with them because they were our good friends and some were like family since we had known each other since before our daughters were born. Many of them I had known for over 6 years. All of them had watched our daughters grow since birth. They were kind, and our friendships had evolved from living next door to each other and spending quality time with them. We each had a wonderful insight to the other's background and had shared many life stories and lessons we had all learned throughout the years. Most of our neighbors were older than us and had lived there years before we had moved in. Collectively, and throughout the years, they offered advice and shared their words of wisdom in a manner that let us know that they truly cared for us. I thought I wasn't ready to see them, but thanks to seeing my *mijas'* smiles that were contagious, they convinced me that it would be okay.

That day I learned from Faye and Josie that they watched Juan work late on our home roof for many late evenings until it was very dark. They shared that on one particular evening our neighbors gathered outside in the middle of the street as a group and yelled out to Juan to get down from the roof. They said it was late in the night and they noticed that he was alone and had been up there for several hours pounding with his hammer and he had been there from the time he had arrived home from work. He resisted at first, but my neighbors finally convinced him to get down from the roof, and he accepted dinner with our neighbors.

I was moved to learn that they had all held hands in a circle and prayed over Juan that evening in the middle of the street. That was a defining moment because Juan finally shared tears among our special friends and neighbors. Juan, a shy and private person, was finally getting the support that he needed. He did not consider himself a religious person. Josie said he walked in the circle and closed his eyes while they prayed over him. Juan hadn't shared this with me.

Our neighbors represent a diversity of cultures and religious beliefs. Picturing them gathered in a circle in the middle of the street and praying over Juan, who I knew was having a difficult time while I was away, soothed me. I was so grateful for those that surrounded him that night and also for the beautiful welcome back home.

Hearing my *mijas* giggle, their soft voices and especially their confidence as their natural instinct was for us to be outside like before, made me realize that their innocence and love was transparent. At that very young age, they already knew how to express their feelings and show me what they felt.

Both girls wanted to hurry up and include some of our closest friends to be with us. I thought how beautiful it felt to witness their confidence and communication resulting in them expressing what we were going to do next. How far back do children remember, I pondered. Did they recall when they were babies and that we all took turns holding them in our arms since they were a few days old and that they had known the girls since birth? Was that an impossibility? Now at this young age of almost 3 and 4 they were the welcoming committee in our home. Somehow they managed to share me with those they trusted and those they knew cared about us. I listened and observed my girls and realized they had grown up some more while we lived in separate places during the almost 4 months that had passed rather quickly now it seemed.

On this same day almost instantaneously my girls began to gather their small cups from under the kitchen cabinet. They took turns standing on their favorite cartoon character step stool to reach for their plates from the cabinet while a group of our friends sat in the kitchen and living room conversing and complimenting them for being so well mannered and gracious.

When our neighbors left our home from their short visit, it reminded me of how much I had missed seeing them all and that it felt real good to be back home.

Our *mijas* continued to assist their dad with moving all the higher-level dishes and plates to the lower shelves. This would be easier for all of us to reach. As weeks and months went by, our girls took turns using their customized favorite character step stool to assist with washing dishes as well. They also began helping me with doing the laundry, putting away the cereal, and organizing the closet. Johnnie liked to wash and dry the dishes, and Jacqueline preferred to be responsible for stacking them neatly in the cupboard. We played music and sang while we separated the clothing that needed washing. As I introduced them to doing the laundry with me, Johnnie separated all the whites, while Jacqueline separated all the colors. I taught them to learn the difference between separating the heavy clothes from the delicate clothing. For example, the heavy jeans and jackets went together, and Mama's light dresses go in the colorful pile with their soft T-shirts and dresses.

Before I knew it, they had mastered washing clothes that needed to be washed in the delicate cycle, and they knew how to separate their dad's heavy jeans in one big pile. They knew that all of the white socks and Daddy's white T-shirts went together in one pile to be washed. The final test to see if my girls were understanding the important process of textures and separating clothes was when I asked them to close their eyes and feel the texture of the clothing. I wanted them to feel the heaviness of the jeans and the lightness of their soft clothes.

We sat for hours at a time on the living-room floor folding clothes and folding the bathroom towels. We tossed Daddy's white socks that we made into soft white balls which we threw back and forth at each other and caught them. The girls also went to the stairs and stood on each stair while we counted out loud the number of that stair as they went up and down to teach them how to count and make learning a fun experience for them.

They took turns carrying a few towels or clothes up the stairs with one hand while holding on to the rail with the other. I watched every step and was intrigued to witness how they had learned patience and coordination when they folded the bathroom towels and had separated the kitchen towels in another pile. We sang rhymes and counted: One, two, three, four, five, six, seven, eight, nine, ten...fourteen! Fourteen meant they had reached the top hallway or had reached me downstairs. We associated each step with a kiss for a total of 14 kisses. I reminded them that both of them were born on the fourteenth day of the month—born on different months, 15 months apart, but they shared that special number 14.

When they walked back downstairs, we counted together backward: fourteen, thirteen...four, three, two, one. Singing in harmony that we were all one family as they reached step number one! We clapped as they took turns going up and down the stairs. Their chores were fun activities that we did together, rhyming or singing that began and ended with a big kiss from Mama!

When I cooked pasta, I showed them how to know if the pasta was ready by throwing a strand of spaghetti on the wall and testing it after

I had boiled it for a few minutes. If the spaghetti stuck to the wall, that meant that the pasta was ready. So naturally, in amazement and eagerness to test this, we grabbed a bunch of stands of spaghetti and threw it on the walls. Taking their job rather seriously they shouted back, "Yup, Mama, spaghetti is ready. Look over there and over there," as they pointed to different sides of the wall where the spaghetti was still stuck there.

We prepared delicious salads and sandwiches and experimented with flavors they enjoyed. They set the table with bright colorful plates while music in English or Spanish played in the background that sometimes motivated us to dance. Their favorite meal that we prepared together was deviled egg sandwiches. After the eggs were boiled and I placed them in cool water, they took turns peeling the eggs. They listened to Mama's instructions and peeled the hardboiled eggs ever so gently. Once they had rinsed them in cold water, they placed them in a bowl where they took turns to mash them. They would repeat out loud everything they heard me say: "Add mustard, mayonnaise, salt and pepper." At the age of now 3 and almost 5 they had learned to make the best egg sandwiches, wash clothes, and organize their toys. They mimicked Mama's voice while already having their own identity that was so different from each other.

They understood that by 7:30 p.m. it was time for bed and "off to sleep with their guardian angels" is what I frequently said to them. I reassured them that their guardian angels would surround them while they rested and fell asleep. They slept in their own beds across from each other in the upstairs bedroom across the hall from our master bedroom.

They understood the importance of expressing what they felt and how important it was that we took turns to listen and speak. We shared our thoughts and our possessions. I gave them examples related to the importance of sharing their toys or books. We took turns to read or share their items with their cousins and friends too. I gave them permission to use my stuff that they found interesting, such as my shoes or pots and pans to play with, as long as they kept everything clean and returned the items in the manner that it was given to them.

They had the freedom to ask any questions that entered their mind and transform the living room and kitchen area into a forest or a castle by the beach. Our rooms were frequently transformed to an exotic and colorful beach or an interesting and magical new space. They found creative ways throughout the house and outside to build and change the appearance of where their new play area was or where they would take a nap. It was intriguing to me to see their imagination and creativity. I watched them amused or in deep concentration.

Johnnie borrowed the sheets from my bed and used them to turn the table and chairs into a castle. Jacqueline banged on the pots and pans that made music while we danced to whatever beat moved us. I used a manual wheelchair in the house or a desk chair with wheels. Sometimes we would sit on the floor for hours at a time while I shared stories with messages that I felt would trigger a conversation or an idea that they thought was important or good. I made it a daily routine to give instructions about the many lessons I wanted them to know about.

Hearing their dialogues about what they liked or didn't like or what they found interesting reminded me of how quickly a child is ready to explore and develop, given the opportunity to have many experiences, and especially when having someone to share with. I was glad that they had each other.

In my own private thoughts I sometimes felt worried and wondered how long I would be able to keep up with my girls, especially when my legs were weak and not strong enough to walk for long periods at a time. I would get tired fast, dizzy, and my body would sweat. This was my sign to sit down and rest. Some days I would have to hold on to the walls and furniture to get my balance or keep me from falling again. Every time I felt weakness in my legs or felt dizzy was a reminder to me that I had to teach my girls all I could, as soon as I could, because I didn't know how long I could. Therefore, I got strength from them as they asked me more questions and they showed me again how much they had learned by my example.

I wanted to capture everything I saw them do and remember every funny question or simple smile as I saw them do an act of kindness that came from them and not because I told them so. I was reminded that one day, I could lose my cognitive skills and forget or lose my voice and not be able to tell them stories or sing to them. I made sure that music, laughter, and singing was a part of our daily routine.

Sometimes, I could still envision my dear neighbor who used to sit at her front bay window and watch us play outside. When I opened my blinds in the morning and faced her home, even though she had passed away from MS complications and was no longer living there, I sometimes remembered her and thanked God that I had another day to give my girls more love and teach them one more lesson. I didn't know how much time I would have to be around them; to smell their sweat from when they ran around in the yard or how many more years I would be able to hear their laughter or watch them grow.

One summer day we were bringing in the groceries from the car. I tripped and fell again. I hit myself hard on the cement. Both girls ran toward me to help me up while I laughed and said, "Oh no, go catch those oranges that want to go visit Frank's house!" They immediately went to rescue the fruit and washed them when we went inside. They enjoyed eating all kinds of fruits while they sat in the tub. I assisted them to bathe or watched them bathe together while they enjoyed eating a big juicy mango in the tub filled halfway with water. I thought that was the perfect place for them to eat mangos. They could have sticky hands, spill the juice in the water, and wipe their hands and their faces if they liked, or let it be sticky. I would peel the fruit halfway so that they could each hold a half-peeled mango and enjoy it in the tub filled with warm water.

A special memory was the day that they were enjoying their juicy mango and Johnnie immediately stopped eating and said, "Mama, listen." "What?" I said. She said, "Listen, Mama, they are playing my song to you." I listened more carefully and I could hear an upbeat song playing in the background on the radio. I heard the English and happy dance style beat. The lyrics were repeated again, "Every time I see you falling, I get down on my knees and pray." I began to laugh and realized that we danced to this song before but didn't really listen to the lyrics. I pictured the different places that I had fallen down, inside our house and outside in public places. Whenever I fell and the girls were present I would say something funny and laugh. Maybe that was my nervous side that came out. I didn't want them to feel bad or sad. I would feel a little embarrassed if others saw. However, it would be hard to tell because before you knew it, I was back up smiling. I always found sometime funny to say.

My girls never cried when they saw me fall. Instead, they were alert and helped with whatever needed picking up and they were ready for the message that I would share after a fall. For example, *"No matter how many times you fall down, don't stay down."* Other times when I would fall the message would be, *"You can stay down as long as you wish, but remember, you have the choice to get up"* or *"Remember that if you fall and you need help, you can ask for help, okay?"* "Yes, Mama" was their response. No matter what the message was, their response would be, "Okay, yes, Mama," and we continued with our activity and went on about our day.

Another time we were at a crowded community fair at the convention center. I was trying to get through the massive crowd while Juan held each girl by their hands in front of me, trying to make a clear path for me to follow in my electric scooter. A young boy possibly 6 years old came running toward me from my right side. I was forced to stop abruptly because crowds of people had crossed over quickly in front of me while I was trying to follow my family.

The child came toward me. I had stopped and was waiting for the crowd to pass by. At that moment, the young boy began to kick my front tires for no apparent reason. The child's parents who were walking still at a distance toward us in the crowd of people began to laugh as they watched in amusement. When I asked him to stop, he kicked harder at my electric scooter. The boy was now also attempting to push my horn and attempted to grab the joystick level that was positioned on my left handrail. The joystick was a hand device that I pushed with minimum force with my left hand. The joystick enabled my electric scooter to have the power to travel faster or slower. I told the child that it was not nice of him to kick my tires, and I asked him again to stop. He continued to kick some more and even harder until I told him, "Would you like me to go find your toys and kick them?" He thought about it, stopped, and walked backward and turned to face his parents, who were *still laughing* at the incident that was not at all funny to my family or me.

Another time, my family and I were inside an elevator with a woman who looked at my girls and said to them, "I am so sorry for you," then asked my husband, "What is wrong with her?" (referring to me sitting in my electric scooter next to my family). I smiled at her and said, "We are all fine, thank you." She wasn't expecting me to respond. We talked about how sometimes people get confused and think that because I was using a wheelchair that meant I was unable to comprehend or communicate. Maybe the stranger just felt uncomfortable looking at me. Therefore, instead, people like her just focus on talking about me in front of me and preferred to have a conversation instead with my husband or the children. The feeling made me feel like I was not present or did not exist. Imagine how many times this same scenario happens to many who are traveling in their wheelchair alone and frequently, strangers would rather turn away and not look at you, or if they did look at you, they gave you a look of pity because that is what they felt.

I ask that we take time to notice strangers passing by you. If they look different or if they have an apparent disability or wheel past you, please take a moment to smile or say hello. This act of kindness could be the one thing that makes them happy that day. Feeling acknowledged goes a long way, and the more of us that do this means more people are coming out from the dark or from those feelings of isolation.

It was disturbing to hear strangers share their regrets or apologies because Juan had a spouse who was disabled or when they expressed sentiments of disappointment because my daughter's mother was ill or sorry that she had to use a wheelchair. Some strangers got confused and thought that somehow me sitting in a wheelchair meant that I couldn't speak, or worse, that my brain didn't work either or that I couldn't talk or had the ability to speak or respond to a question. Yes, we as a community can be naïve, ignorant, have stereotypes, and impose biases. Assumptions about a person living with a disability and who many times have many abilities are shadowed or made to feel invisible or not important enough to be acknowledged for the simple fact that the person is sitting in a wheelchair or because the person displays an apparent physical limitation or intellectual disability.

The most disturbing incident that I experienced was not when I was sitting in my wheelchair. I was actually standing in line (wearing my leg braces which were invisible because they were hidden by my long dress. As I stood in the grocery store line with my daughters, two ladies in front of me began to talk about me in Spanish out loud to each other. They were accusing me of being a drug addict and shame on me! Then they were almost shouting with the persons behind me who also joined in to say that I was an unfit mother because they noticed that my hands were shaking and so were parts of my body while I stood in line in between them merely waiting my turn to pay for the groceries.

At first I thought they were talking about someone else, so I looked around me and behind me to see if I noticed a person who appeared to look like a drug addict. Then their negative vibes toward me told me that they were talking about me. Yes, they viewed me as an unfit mother and said in Spanish that my children should be taken away from me. When my eyes met theirs, it reaffirmed to me that they were talking about me. I felt their mean glares and negative energy.

In disbelief of what was happening my first thought was to tell them off. I took a deep breath, and then I looked straight back at them with anger on my face as I felt my body boil with rage. The lady told me to my face, "Shame on you!" (*¡Qué lástima!*) I felt my body ignite. I could not stay quiet. I was upset and yelled back that I was not a drug addict and they had no right to judge me. I could have said a lot more, but somehow, I was able to refrain from doing what my first reaction was to do. Instead, I told myself, this is a teaching moment. I wanted to set a good example for my daughters versus shouting vulgar words that almost came out of my mouth as a result of feeling attacked and bullied. I decided I didn't have to share or justify myself with these ignorant strangers about my diagnosis, or give them an explanation as to why my body and hands were shaking. It wasn't any of their business. I did not feel that I had to justify myself. However, since my daughters were with me, I felt strongly that I had to at least say something, especially because I had told them in previous communication that we have to stand up for ourselves when we think we are right and say what you believe to be true.

The first words that I thought were to attack them and say nasty words back and defend myself. But instead, I blurted out in Spanish, "¡*Basta!* (Stop!) You have no right to judge me." The person in line in front of me and behind us stopped at the same time as I said it loud again, enough for all in the line to hear. They continued to give me that look of disappointment or disgust. In their mind, I was a drug addict. During that time I was taking a new treatment drug for multiple sclerosis, and the side effect that I experienced were flulike symptoms and shaking throughout my body that also led to my liver being affected. Ultimately, I discontinued this treatment medication. I thought, *How could medicine that was supposed to help me get better affect my vital organ, my liver?* I didn't drink or smoke and for my blood test to show that my liver blood results keep coming back abnormal concerned me. I didn't comprehend how something that was supposed to help me get better made we feel worse and was attacking my liver.

I made the decision to discontinue the MS treatment medication despite the doctor's recommendation to give it 6 more months. I listened, instead, to my body and my sister Jackie that pleaded with me to stop, as she couldn't bear to see me experience these horrible side effects that never got better. Guess what? My liver results went back to normal once I stopped taking the medication that my body rejected.

**"A mother's love is like no other. A child's love is everything."
Simply Amor**

Chapter 8

My Sister Jackie

*M*y sister Jacqueline (Jackie) and I are 11 months apart. I am her older sister. We had been close since childhood. Of course, we have had our disagreements and our arguments almost on a daily basis when we were growing up. However, for the most part, we did everything together and still do. My sister Jackie followed my lead. The way she looked up to me was similar to the way that we also both looked up to our older sister Debbie. Jacqueline was the youngest of the three daughters. I was the middle sister. When Juan and I got married at the courthouse, my sister Debbie was our witness and we selected her as the godmother *(madrina)* to Johnnie when she was baptized. My sis Jacqueline was selected as the godmother *(madrina)* to both of my daughters who were baptized in the Catholic church when they were infants and witnessed by our family and closest friends. My youngest daughter Jacqueline was named after her nina-godmother Jacqueline.

As soon as I was admitted to the hospital on that Mother's Day weekend, my sisters were there for my family, and they took on the godmother or sister role rather seriously. During this time of our family crisis, my sister Jacqueline (Jackie) was employed at one of the largest oil companies. She was fully invested in the company and had all the perks that came with working for a big company for over 14 years. She confided in me and my husband Juan while I was in the intensive care unit that she would quit her job and move into our home in order to assist with caring for our children or move in and continue working and assist Juan and me with the many financial needs that were piling up. My sis Jackie put us first before herself. We did not expect this unconditional act of love.

We shared a mutual love for her and felt strongly that despite her genuine wanting to put us before herself, we could not allow her to quit her job and move in with us to help us. We felt that Jackie deserved to live a life of her own, get married, and have her own children one day. She deserved to be a mommy like our sis Debbie and me.

My husband Juan and Jackie had mutual admiration for each other and sister Jackie appreciated Juan being the big brother to her who was always there to assist her with whatever she needed as best he could. If it meant Juan driving her and her sick cat to the emergency animal hospital late at night then he rushed out of bed to take her because we did not want her to drive or go alone, especially in the middle of the night. If something broke and needed fixing in her house, or if her car needed an oil change or tire fixed, Juan took care of it.

Naturally I did my best to be there for my sister Jackie too, and like her, there wasn't anything that I wouldn't do for her if I could. It was especially beautiful to witness the special bond between Juan and my sister. Growing up without a brother and seeing that Juan filled that role with my sister Jackie made me very happy. A union that was built on trust, respect, and knowing that no matter what, we were always there for each other. I guess you can say that what we felt for each other was mutual, and it wasn't until I was in this position of desperation and fear of the unknown that I really knew how special this relationship was.

Before my hospital stay, I was the big sister that looked out for my sis Jackie. Now that I needed my sister more than ever, she was there to ensure that my girls continued with their routine and normalcy while I recovered at the hospital. She was now the big sister. During this period, my sister Jackie was not married. She did not have children of her own and our daughters filled that role. In her eyes, the best solution was that we pull together and count on each other during this new adjustment of me now having some physical limitations or unexpected health problems.

Despite the challenges of me being away at the hospital had caused in her personal life, my sister was ready to put her life on hold in order to support my family and me. She took time off from work to assist my husband and our parents with caring for our daughters. Naturally, prior to this time, my sis was very much involved in our lives. However, now it was different because I needed her to make sure that our girls were doing fun and happy activities while Mama was away at the hospital and Dad was working. Not to say that my husband wouldn't do what he could.

The relationship between my sister and me was different from that of my husband and me. Yes, Juan had to work to continue with monthly bills that wouldn't stop or go away simply because now our life was changed. We still had the monthly mortgage house payment and need to return to a normal routine for our girls. Juan took care of our daughters too, but there was a special connection that sisters and mamas had. Thank goodness for my sisters and my mama that reinforced that our daughters were not alone.

My sister Jackie had cleared her schedule so that every week she would pick up our girls from my mom and keep them for a few days before they went home to spend time with their daddy while I was recovering at the hospital. She prepared their dinner, brought goodies, played with them and cuddled them before they got ready for bed. She took them to the beach and swimming and did activities with them that kept them preoccupied and filled with moments of fun. Juan worked long days and when he ended his work schedule at the end of a long day, he continued to work on our house that was still under construction or he was back at the hospital to visit with me.

My sister Debbie was supportive too. I took into consideration that she had a family of her own to look after. I am forever grateful and thankful to her too for being there at whatever capacity she could for my girls and me. Thank you, sister Debbie!

Thanks to our extended families, as well, our girls were kept together. It was important for me that they not be separated because they were close, and I did not want them to miss each other or grow apart. Sometimes our girls stayed at my mom's, my sister Jackie, or at home with their dad depending on his work schedule and our extended family's rotation time. It was reassuring to know that between both of our families, Juan's and mine, our daughters were in good hands.

Juan and our family brought the girls to visit me at the rehabilitation hospital at least three times a week, and during the weekends we spent a lot of time together in the outside area that had grass and tables and privacy for us to spend the day together. My sis Jackie would take our girls to the mall, movies, beach, and swimming. My sis soon became my *mijas'* second mommie while Mama was away. A special bond was formed with my daughters and their nina Jackie that is even stronger today.

"Unconditional love has no limits." Simply Amor

Chapter 9

My Sadness

*F*rom the outside it appeared that I was adjusting well with living with the diagnosis of multiple sclerosis. However, inside, I felt an uncertainty because I didn't know from one day to the next how my body was going to feel. And the not knowing of how quickly I would progress scared me. I thought about Margo secretly and who had since passed away from MS complications. I kept my feelings private because after all, I had a wonderful family and support system. I wasn't supposed to feel sad. I had many reasons to be happy is what I continued to tell myself.

I kept all my different outpatient appointments at the rehabilitation center. The outpatient physical therapy provided treatment for my legs, the orthopedic doctor modified the large metal braces to AFO braces that were lighter and made of plastic with Velcro straps that adjusted below my knees. I no longer used the arm metal braces or the heavy leg braces that went up to my thighs.

My right foot would drop unexpectedly occasionally; causing me to fall that resulted in bruises or scrapes on my body, depending on how I landed. Sometimes I got bloody kneecaps from scrapes on the pavement or my wrist would hurt from the falls I took when I used my hands to protect myself when I fell. This happened more frequently when I walked for more than a few hours at a time, like when I went to the market or ran errands. I had to take breaks in between.

Sometimes a simple task of carrying groceries or other items caused me to lose my balance or feel dizzy. I didn't like to close my eyes when I took a shower for fear of falling again. The weird thing was that I could have great days and weeks without tripping and my legs were strong enough to walk without having to use the wheelchair all the time. I knew ahead of time when it was time to rest. I used the wheelchair as needed. My body would show me signs to slow down.

When my legs felt weak and I would feel dizzier or exhausted, especially in the summer months, I rested more. I avoided the heat and stayed indoors or in cool places when I could because the heat exacerbated my condition and drained me of my energy. I tried to only use the wheelchair when I absolutely had to and relied more on my leg braces.

When at home, I liked sitting on a desk chair with wheels instead of the wheelchair. I carefully selected my clothes so that my leg braces could easily go under my loose pants. I wore long, colorful dresses that covered my leg braces. I didn't like to be photographed; instead, I was the one that liked to take the photos and capture the memories. If I was going to be in a photo my family knew that the leg braces and wheelchair were to be moved away from the photograph or the photo was taken waist high so that the focus would not be the metal or plastic leg braces, and I would transfer from the wheelchair to the couch when there was a photo opportunity. Juan hid away the arm metal braces in the attic when he noticed I didn't need them anymore, or maybe because he didn't like to see them.

The neurologist at the rehabilitation hospital followed my treatment and I continued with muscle relaxers for the spasms, amantadine for energy, and took steroids when the doctor said I was having an episode or exacerbation (onset of a symptom or progression of MS).

During one of my doctor visits, the neurologist at the MS clinic asked me to consider having permanent cauterization. That meant that I would have a surgery performed so that I would only urinate by using a catheter. She explained that it would be an easy procedure and convenient so that I would not have to rely on the use of an adult diaper or have urinary accidents. I refused this surgery because I did not want to believe that I was getting worse. I wanted to believe that I was getting better. So what if I had a few accidents with peeing? The adult diaper helped, and I was doing muscle-strengthening exercises that may help to improve this sensitive issue. I didn't want to have a bag filled with pee hanging on the side of my clothing.

I knew that some of the patients at the hospital complained of bladder infections and how uncomfortable it made them feel. And how would this affect my sexual intimacy with Juan? I still didn't want to get close to Juan in this manner. It was still too soon, and I didn't feel sexy anymore. Having a permanent catheter would definitely remind me that I was getting worse.

Meanwhile, my sister Jackie continued to come around more frequently and sometimes she came by when we were out running errands. She had the key to our house and oftentimes she left groceries or goodies in the refrigerator or left surprise gifts for the girls. She liked to surprise us like that. When we would return home she had already left. A thoughtful and humbling gesture that I received and was thankful for, but it also reminded me of what I wasn't doing for my family. My mixed feelings of fear, frustration, despair, denial, then hope, happiness, and contentment would come and go and living across from where Ms. Margo used to sit was a thought that would enter my mind. I started to keep the blinds closed that faced her window. I didn't feel like socializing with my neighbors as much as before. I spent more time inside with my girls and did my best to show them that I was okay.

I prepared in advance to go to my doctor appointments, rested the night before, and saved my strength for the long day at the clinic. I didn't like to inconvenience my husband to go with me. Besides, the day at the MS clinic would be long, and Juan's work in construction was sometimes slow so when he had work, I preferred that he work instead. The hospital bills continued to pile up, and I wasn't working. I felt his stress. Now he had more roles at home. Even though he didn't complain, I could see his sadness and worry. This was another reason why I preferred that he didn't travel with me to my medical appointments. I knew that this environment would make him feel worse, so in my own way, I protected him and made believe that I was okay traveling to my appointments without him. He didn't know that I dreaded going to them and wished he would accompany me.

On one particular day, I packed some healthy snacks for my girls, put on my leg braces, and put my manual wheelchair in the trunk of my car. Off we went, my girls and I, to the rehabilitation clinic for my outpatient appointment. I parked at the back entrance as usual, brought down my wheelchair from the trunk, and proceeded to enter the hospital facility with my girls next to me. My girls knew the routine already for when we traveled in the community without my husband. They held hands and walked close to Mama. Jacqueline was walking in the middle holding the side of my wheelchair and her sister's hand. We were about to enter the rehabilitation hospital electronic clear doors that swung open. Jacqueline immediately stopped in her tracks and pulled me back away from the electronic doors and entrance to the hospital. She cried out and begged me, "Mama, I don't like going in there! Mama, let's go home now. Please, let's not go in there!" I was confused, surprised, and sad to see her so out of control. She was quiet in the car on the way over there. I didn't realize until that moment how much she was still emotionally affected by the experience of having to return to the hospital again. Despite my reassurance that I was only going to see the doctor for a short time and that we would all go home together on that day, she did not seem to listen or comprehend that this time the stay would be only for a little while.

I did not make her go inside. I stopped, turned around, and the three of us went by the shade to talk. After I calmed her down in my arms, I kissed her. I reassured her that she would not ever have to return there again if she didn't want to. I told her that I would have to go in to the hospital but just for a little while as an outpatient, which meant I was coming back out today. I said to her once more that I was going to sleep at home tonight and that this appointment was different because the doctor would only check me, and then we would all go home like the last time we came. I tried to remind her of the previous appointment when she last came with me and her sister for my outpatient appointment. Somehow, from the last time that we came to this time, she had made the decision that she would not enter anymore.

I immediately contacted Juan's parents who lived just a few miles away. My father-in-law came immediately and took the girls to their home and they waited there for me while I continued with my outpatient appointment. From that day on, I never again took my *mijas* with me to my doctor appointments. I made arrangements ahead of time and dropped them off so that they could visit with their *abuelito* and *abuelita* or other family members while I returned for my doctor appointments.

On another occasion, Juan was able to get home early from work and stay with the girls so that I could make the two appointments that I had that particular afternoon. My first appointment that day was with a neurologist who told me that I should not drive anymore due to my foot dropping. She encouraged me to use my wheelchair more to avoid the falling accidents after she observed the bruises on my kneecaps. She said again that I could prevent my falling accidents if I used the wheelchair more. I pleaded for another solution because I could not imagine myself not driving my girls to daily fun activities and stressed to her that this didn't happen every day. I did not want to rely on others to drive us around. She asked me to rest more. I shared that my foot only dropped sometimes and that my feet were strong enough to drive. I experienced the foot drop only when I walked for long periods at a time, and I always listened to my body and rested or sat and wouldn't drive if my feet or legs were weak. I would never drive if I felt I couldn't.

She then reminded me also about the permanent cauterization procedure that I was against having. She asked if I had changed my mind and if I was ready to have this procedure scheduled. I gave her the same response: "No, I do not want surgery for permanent cauterization." I was in agreement with her that sometimes it was difficult to rest more with little ones that needed my full attention at all times. However, I also knew my body and its limitations, and I really believed I was improving. I told her again that, "No, I would not agree to a permanent cauterization procedure that would prevent me from peeing like I do now." If I agreed to this procedure, it meant that the area of where I urinated would be sewed up and a hole for the tube connected to a catheter bag would be with me permanently and I would have to empty the bag manually every time it got full of urine.

I left the neurology clinic feeling frustrated and questioned if I really knew what was best for me. I was trying to be hopeful with my prognosis, and yet, the neurologist's observation of me was that I was getting worse.

I made it on time to my next appointment that afternoon that was downstairs in the basement. It was with the eye doctor, an ophthalmologist. He studied my optic nerve and shared that my left eye seemed to show a thinning of the nerve fibers. He said, "Don't worry about it now," but it was something that I needed to keep an eye on to ensure that the eyeball would not detach. He talked slow and in a serious manner. He described how nerve fibers and tissues held the eyeball and how all of our nerves connect and communicated with our brain. He shared how sometimes the eyeball detached, and how some people living with MS become blind due to the central nervous system possibly causing nerve damage to the eye. He said a lot more of what could happen or what was known to happen to some individuals with the diagnosis of MS.

By now, I was lost in my own thoughts. I remembered how difficult it was at first for me to start walking again with the assistance of the physical therapist, and then with the leg braces. I remembered how initially, I walked like a robot because it took time for my brain to communicate with my legs.

The eye doctor interrupted my thoughts by putting his hands in front of me and pulled them away to demonstrate his example. "Like gum when it is chewed and you pull it away, and finally the gum detaches or separates when pulled apart; well, that's what can happen to your eye." He continued speaking, "You didn't know that sometimes MS could cause a person to lose their vision?" I responded, "No I didn't know that." I left the examining room without further communication and without scheduling my return appointment.

I rushed out of the hospital with a heavy sadness and wheeled out of the facility as quickly as I could go. I placed my wheelchair in the trunk and missed the freeway entrance. I decided to get back home by traveling by the streets and not the freeway. As I drove home, I thought about how my right foot would sometime drop forward and how that could be dangerous if I somehow lost strength in my legs or feet when driving. I thought of my girls and how I would want to keep them safe and free from harm. Even though today my legs were stronger and I felt strong enough to drive and they were home safe with their daddy, could I possibly lose my strength when driving? Oh my God, I hadn't thought of that happening since this had never occurred. Was I being ignorant and not really getting better? I questioned myself and wasn't sure if I would really know if my legs were too weak to drive. Was my stubbornness and ego interfering with my judgment and putting others at risk? A part of me was in conflict because I knew that the right foot drop was hard to gauge because if I knew ahead of time, why had I fallen so many times? Okay, so the doctor had a point. She was correct. I didn't know in advance for sure when my right foot would drop, even though I was pretty good at knowing that when my legs were weak it meant that there was a chance my foot would drop; therefore, this was my signal to rest. However, I pushed myself many times, and I did not want to admit that I was not being safe.

Now learning that I should not drive—hearing again about the strong recommendation for permanent cauterization—and now learning that I may also lose my sight—devastated me. I felt that this was the last straw of bad news that I could take.

I felt helpless. I tried to process this as I was driving home. I pictured myself blind. I thought of my beautiful girls and how difficult that would be for them to have a mom that would probably progress with MS and forget them like Ms. Margo did her daughters. My cries turned to aches as I drove home. I did not want to lose my vision. I wanted to see my girls grow up. I wanted to drive them to the park and watch them play together and witness their expressions of curiosity as they studied the gorillas and the elephants at the zoo. I wanted to be in control of my life. I did not want to be a burden to Juan and my children. They deserved a better mama, and Juan, well, Juan was handsome, a nice guy, and I thought he would be okay if I was gone, and in time, he would find someone else to love. Maybe he already stopped loving me and was only with me out of pity . . .

I loved my girls so much, but they deserve better than this. I loved Juan enough to let him go for a better wife and life. I was affecting their future, and I wanted them to have a better life. Juan was not sharing his feelings lately, and I imagined that he was unhappy and probably wanted to leave me but felt that he had to stay for the sake of the girls. I thought of my sister Jackie, who was not married. I knew how much she loved my girls and Juan too. Was this a sign for me to see that my sister, who loved my girls and Juan so much, and who was not married and had no children...Maybe she was supposed to be the one to raise them...Maybe there was a reason for why she hadn't found the right man. Maybe she wasn't supposed to have children because she was supposed to raise mine. She was the godmother to both of them, after all. I pictured Juan and my sister together if I was gone. I knew that she would be a great mama. She had already proven that with my girls and the love my children and she expressed to each other was beautiful.

At that very moment, I felt that I did not want to live anymore. I wanted to give up. I wanted to die instantly in a car accident like I had seen on the news. At that very moment, while 20 minutes from my home driving down a little hill, instead of stopping at the next light that had turned red, I pushed on the gas and sped up, and then stopped abruptly in the middle of the street near the freeway while the cars driving from right to left were moving fast toward me. My stopped vehicle was in the middle of the street. I closed my eyes and cried out in my mind, "God, please take me!" I heard honking and opened my eyes to see that cars were driving around me. No cars had hit me. I sat in my car, still located in the middle of the street. I could not believe that I had done this. I was crying uncontrollably, and my entire body was shaking.

By this time a man was banging on my front window and was cursing me in English and Spanish. His car door was wide open and positioned a short distance from mine. His last words were, "You crazy lady, you could have killed someone." I managed to drive away without a scratch and no one or any vehicles were affected.

I immediately drove under the freeway underpass and parked at the first place that I could. I stopped in front of a house that had a space open for me to park. I sat there for over an hour and replayed what had just happened. I thought of how stupid and—yes—crazy—of me to put others at risk. What was I thinking? I did not want to harm anyone. It was never my intent to harm anyone. At that moment—yes, I wanted to disappear. I was irrational and didn't think through what I was doing. I cried until I was exhausted. I felt that my soul and happy spirit were gone or lost. I knew that I was depressed but had never known this type of depression before. I also knew that I needed help. I was ashamed of what I had just done and how it would have been worse if I had harmed innocent people. How would I live with myself? What would my daughters think of their mom being stupid and nuts? I did not like who I had become. My selfish act could have had a horrible outcome. Thank God that I did not harm anyone.

I finally got the courage to drive myself home with shame and guilt for what I had become. How dare me! I had everything—a great husband and two daughters that loved me and needed me. My trip from the rehabilitation hospital to my home usually took me around 35 minutes. On this day, I was almost 2 hours late getting home.

When I entered my home Juan was playing with the girls in the living room. I told myself that I would not share this embarrassing incident. Juan and the girls couldn't tell that I was nuts. The house was in order, my daughters were calmly playing together, and Juan came walking toward me and kissed me. I stood silent for a moment. He asked if I had stopped to see my mom since he noticed I was late. I responded, "No, I wanted to die today."

He looked at me and said, "You don't mean that, do you?"

I said, "Honey, I did something horrible. I ran a red light and stopped in the middle of the street and waited for cars to hit me, but no one hit me. I told God that I wanted to die."

He grabbed me in his arms and said, "What are you saying? How could you think of leaving me, leaving your girls?"

I replied, "You deserve better than me. The doctor said that I shouldn't drive because of my foot drop. I may have to wear a diaper all the time or have a surgery for permanent cauterization, and the eye doctor said I could lose my vision, a side effect that happens sometimes with people having MS. I may go blind, and I am scared...if I can't see my girls grow up...I understand if you want to leave me . . ." I blurted out, "I want you to marry my sister. She is prettier than I and doesn't have MS. I love her, and she loves you, and she is the godmother to both of our girls...and she doesn't wear a diaper."

Juan replied in a sad and low voice, "I do not love your sister like that. I love you, and I'm never going to leave you, until death do us part, remember?...We will be together a long time, honey, no matter what. We will get through this together."

I melted in his arms and cried like a scared child. I let him see the real me, and I knew at that moment that he still wanted me. After I calmed down, I thought again of my selfish act. How stupid I was. I began to pray by myself like I had never prayed in my life. I told God that I knew that I was not a religious person, but I believed that he was with me, especially today. I felt his presence protect me during the incident where all the cars were going fast and how they all missed me. I finally acknowledged his presence. I thanked God for protecting me.

I played back my moment of desperation and could not believe what I had done and what my mind wanted to do. It was like I was seeing someone else drive in the traffic. How could I have been capable of such ugly thoughts, wanting to leave this earth? I hadn't thought it through because if I rationalized it and pictured me harming someone else, I don't believe that I would have gone through with what my mind wanted to do. It scared me to think that this incident could have had a very different outcome. This was for sure the lowest point in my life.

God knew that I did not wish to harm anyone. I just wanted out. This was too hard. I was terrified and a wimp. I really thought at that moment of insanity while I was rushing into the traffic that I would die instantly. That's how I kept playing it in my head. I even pictured Juan sad, but then he would be relieved, and then live happily ever after with my beautiful sister. Yes, they would miss me at first for a while, but then he would be okay. My repeated thoughts after leaving the rehabilitation hospital that day were that my sister would be the best mother to raise my girls. My sister deserved them. I didn't feel worthy enough for them.

As I replayed what I had contemplated, I understood how easily a person could lose himself, lose the most important people in his or her life. A feeling of helplessness that came from fear of the unknown...that was rooted in suicidal thoughts...that turned into actions that could have been deadly. This was what major depression was. I had it, and I didn't want it. I asked God for forgiveness for wanting to give up and for all the negative thoughts that overcame me.

That evening, I made a promise to God. I spoke to God and told him that I would never leave my family. I knew at that moment that something inside me changed. I knew that I had felt his love. When I continued to pray I felt stronger and experienced an inner peace. Somehow, without knowing why, I knew that I would never return to this low ugly place again. I knew that God would take me when it was my time to go. I promised God that I would serve him for as long as I could. I told him that I would help other people, especially those that I saw felt isolated and alone, so that they wouldn't give up. I did not want anyone to feel like I had—experiencing that feeling of uncertainty and that there life didn't count.

In my efforts to redeem myself and to become a better person, I gravitated toward longing to reach as many people as I could that needed a friend. I wanted to demonstrate positive energy and give love to anyone that would accept it, and even if they didn't want it, I was going to give it to them anyway! I know this sound corny and possibly out of control. I agree. I became out of control in going in the entirely *different* direction from wanting to end my life. Maybe it was because it was frightening to go back to revisit that horrible past experience. I had to make sure that as long as I could, I would share love and positive energy and hopefully help someone else avoid that dark and evil place.

As I began to heal psychologically, I returned to the rehabilitation center and became a volunteer. I no longer associated thoughts of hospitals as a dark and gloomy place where I used to feel vulnerable and scared. Now, they represented a place where I would bring hope, my resources, or whatever good I could to make a stranger smile. I felt like God was taking me to a happier place. God had given me the gift to know who at the hospital really needed someone to speak to or who needed a positive message.

Many of those that I reached out to I never saw again. I trusted that the smile, hug, listening ear, or good resources that I shared with the patient was exactly what he or she needed and was what I was supposed to give. There was no time to understand it. All I knew was that that I was just getting started and God would guide me to where I needed to be. I was traveling with my faith and left it at that.

Oftentimes, I would scan every place I entered and was moved in certain directions to where I was supposed to be. I shared a smile, a gentle touch, or gave someone that acknowledgment that I felt they needed, and I continued on my journey. I felt a sense of inner peace, and the feeling of love was contagious. The more I gave, the more I wanted to give, one person at a time, every day for my rest of my life is what I told myself in my private thoughts. I vowed to be a family or friend to those who needed one. I told God that I would do my best to be a good mom to my children and a good wife to my husband.

Juan and I never talked again about this incident. I didn't talk about this with my sister either, initially for fear of her disappointment in me. During this time, my sister saw me as courageous—when, in fact, I was a coward. It took me awhile to heal and forgive myself. I carried the shame and regret for some time. This was a period that I prayed away and replaced this incident with working on being the best example that I could for my daughters. I needed to earn their respect and love.

That day at the intersection was the lowest point of my life. A life that I had taken for granted, and finally saw clearly that, no matter what I was going through, I was not going through it alone.

That lowest day of my life was also the time that my spiritual belief in God told me that I was not alone. The message that kept coming to my thoughts was that I had to trust and listen to my gut. That voice that was inside me told me that this was only the beginning of greatness to come and that no matter what happened to me in this new journey with living with multiple sclerosis, I was going to be okay.

I had my husband, my family, and especially, I had somehow finally believed that God had never left me. God had carried me out of my lowest point. I knew I would never want to be that fragile again, or that person that I still find it difficult to believe was I.

In the coming week while I prepared breakfast for my girls, I told them that I was going to show them all I knew. They continued to speak with each other about the cereal box that was almost finished and how cold milk tasted better than warm milk. I interrupted and said that as long as we had a brain that worked, we could do anything we wanted to. They didn't look up and crunched on their cereal, and this told me that they were not really in the mood to talk about a brain when their cereal could get soggy at any given moment. Even though I knew they were not listening or understanding entirely what I was saying, I continued to think of how I could teach them to be independent and loving, and young ladies of character and value. The only thing I could think of that came out of my mouth was to show them. So, I told them that I would teach them by my actions about what it meant to have good values, respect, and that I would teach them about God and his love for them.

They said, "Okay, Mama," not quite sure what I was talking about, but they began to show interest. I am still not sure if they really understood this important speech I was sharing because they looked up only when the cereal was all gone. I wasn't sure if they finally looked because they were finished eating or because a part of what I was saying was capturing their attention. I made every day a teaching moment. I watched them carefully and saw where their personalities were so different. I began to notice their similarities. I observed, shared funny stories and serious ones too, and I loved them with all my heart.

I told myself that if I focused on sharing love, respect, and God, then no matter what happened to me, they would be okay, and so would I. It got to the point that my confidence and spiritual beliefs grounded me and helped me to believe that everything was, indeed, possible. I saw with clarity what I had to do, and this time, there was nothing stopping me. I was no longer afraid. I did not question this new journey anymore. I found peace in knowing that no matter what happened to my health, I knew that there was a positive in every situation if we looked closely enough. I was now on a personal mission, and my path led me to be of service to my family, and my heart was open to anyone that asked for help or anyone that I was moved to support.

With this new sense of purpose and direction, the worst scenario that used to cause me fear, like becoming visually impaired or having limited mobility, was now something that I accepted and I could live with. Why? What changed? I learned that fear had frozen my thoughts and had already crippled my spirit. When I chose life I gave myself choices to heal, and just with that simple thought of telling myself that "I do count, I am valuable," it helped me to see that there were many things that I didn't have control of. However, I could choose to be positive and turn the feeling of fear to a feeling of joy and peace, instead. I kept telling myself that being positive attracted more loving experiences. It is true, I often told myself, "as long as my brain worked and I could conceptualize my thoughts, have a memory to remember who I was when I woke up, that meant that I had another opportunity to try again to be the best I could be for this day."

Naturally, as time passed, I witnessed some friends and family members close to me, and even strangers, experience the loss of their memory due to Alzheimer's, various forms of dementia, or simply because they were getting old and were in the last phase of their life. Witnessing this was sad to see, or even scary for anyone who is getting old, or has a loved one that is already experiencing this. This led me to ask myself, "Who am I to discount that not having a brain that functioned like before was less important?" After all, if we are still alive, under even the worst circumstances, it is for a reason that I may not fully understand.

I decided that focusing on making my daily routine count helped me to redefine my purpose. Regarding my judgment of who I had become or how my final phase of life would turn out, I decided to let go and let God guide me. After all, I had so much to still learn and do. Whatever was to become of my health or how soon I would deteriorate would evolve by itself. Many contributing factors would affect the course of this journey. For example, I needed to take charge of eating healthier and push myself to do more exercises that I knew was not one of my strengths. I gravitated to reaching out to as many positive influences that were already all around me. In other words, do as much as I knew that would bring peace and balance despite this journey of living with MS that was unpredictable, something I would never quite understand. What I did understand was that the MS was not going to take over my life, and I was not going to give up, no matter what.

There were too many exciting things I still wanted to experience. My point is this: I am no longer worrying about when or how I am going to die. I am too busy enjoying my life and learning to be healthier. Therefore, I had rationalized that if I was confined to my bed I could still travel to many beautiful places on the Internet or in my private thoughts, with courage and imagination. If pain or death was to come, then it would come, and that's it. I am not going to live forever and every moment spent with negative worry would mean one moment of not being happy. All I knew for sure was that I loved my family and friends with all my heart. I told myself that my girls would be okay as long as I continued to give them love, teach them about God, and be the best example I could. My daily prayer was that their lives would always be filled with love. I wanted them to feel and believe that, and that their faith would remind them that they would never be alone because with love in their heart, everything and anything was possible.

I felt strongly that no matter what happened to me, they were going to be okay. I didn't carry the burden of worry any longer. I witnessed their confidence, loving actions to people, and their respect for animals and this planet earth that they loved, which demonstrated their innocent actions, and these gave me strength, and more strength, and this is what filled me up each day.

When our daily experiences were shared with conscious expressions of love, those were the times when I was able to see our daughters' individuality, self-esteem, and eagerness to explore. And these times were enhanced by 100 percent. I made a conscious effort to be positive and find the goodness in all experiences despite the challenges that were endured in the process. I communicated with them honestly and with heartfelt conversations that gave them something to think about. I respect their perspective that further enhanced their individuality. They became critical thinkers who communicated their expressions and made decisions to resolve or improve where they continued to evolve. I replaced the word "challenge" to represent "opportunities to grow." I decided not to claim that I had MS. Instead, I said that I was *diagnosed* with MS. I didn't want anyone to see me as a victim or to be referred to as "the lady who was sick or disabled." I was as healthy as I could be. I began to focus more on other aspects of who I was besides that diagnosis of MS. I slowly began to have more energy than ever before.

We started traditions at home that would bring a positive association with my diagnosis of MS. Each year, we took turns picking out the Christmas tree. We also contributed in the kitchen and cooked our favorite dishes for the holidays.

To commemorate how well I was doing with living with MS, we remembered that it was during the month of May and Mother's Day celebration when my life developed new meaning that was initially associated with my diagnosis of MS. However, we decided to continue to make Mother's Day a day a special celebration and not focus on the day that Mama went away for a long time.

As a family, we also started a tradition of planting a rosebush in our yard during Mother's Day. We planned in advance where we would plant another rosebush so that on Mother's Day, we already had the rosebush. We made time to plant it and say a special prayer, giving thanks to God for life and the many blessings that surrounded us. We gave thanks for each other also and for another opportunity to wake up and make it a beautiful day!

Every year we selected another rosebush to plant, a different color and at a different location in the yard. Our front and backyard had beautiful big roses. We learned that our house used to be a farm that had many horses before we had acquired this property. Therefore, the fertilizer from the horses and other animal life that lived here before us had enriched the soil in the entire cul-de-sac area where we lived. This rich history about the soil was perfect nourishment for any kind of plant, and when mixed with a sprinkle of human touch rooted in love, was breathtaking.

One year we realized that we did not have enough space for another rosebush. Therefore, my girls and Juan surprised me by planting a jacaranda tree instead in the front of the house centered away in the opposite direction from the rosebushes. The jacaranda tree was in its infancy stage, and it would grow in the years to come if we took care of it. That day, they made me wait inside the house with all the window blinds closed. I had to promise them that I would not peek out the window or go outside until they called me. What a beautiful surprise to see the tiny purple flowers that were on the little tree branches. My family was all full of dirt and sweaty from digging the deep hole in the grass that Mother's Day that replaced the rosebush tradition. The principle of celebrating life with the planting of a rosebush or tree reminded us of the natural beauty that was all around us and was growing strong with us.

As the girls got older, the special tradition evolved to having fresh flowers inside our home and throughout our house from our garden, beautiful flowers that flourished throughout the years, a reminder that life is beautiful and the colorful flowers and big purple jacaranda tree blooms and grows each year like our love for one another, and the strength that keeps us rooted in our faith.

When my girls were in grade school, I enjoyed volunteering and assisting the teachers with grading papers, reading to the children, and sharing stories and songs that I made up. I kept my leg braces at home or they were under my long dresses if I didn't feel like displaying them. My time at the school was for only a few hours at a time. I used my wheelchair only for long distances as my neurologist reminded me that it was best to conserve my energy and not to push myself to exhaustion.

Mrs. Yoshizaki was a second-grade teacher to both of my daughters. She encouraged me and inspired me to go to college and continue with higher education. She saw me as an educator and role model for the children who looked forward to my funny stories and songs that I made up that told them how special they were.

As I took steps to consider going back to school as an option, I learned that because I had worked over 10 years prior to my diagnosis of MS, I qualified for assistance from the Department of Rehabilitation to return to school and further my education with their support and financial assistance. The Department of Rehabilitation, assisted me and paid for the modifications to my van. They also supported the specialized driver's training so that I could learn to adapt to driving differently with the special instructor who taught me how to drive with a left gas petal instead of using a right gas pedal. I learned how to drive again without the use of my right foot since that was the foot that dropped. It was amusing to me that my brain had told my right foot not to move to push the gas pedal like I did prior to the diagnosis of MS. Now, the only foot that moved when I drove was the left foot that had a left foot gas pedal installed and modified especially for me. This was liberating. My Rehabilitation Counselor – Ms. Edith Hovey always advocated for me to hang in there and would exclaim "one more semester" and reinforced to my daughters the importance of education.

I had to renew my license with the Department of Motor Vehicles and was approved to drive with a disabled placard once I successfully passed my new driving method. I did not use my right foot to drive anymore. This opportunity was made possible because of one special neurologist that supported my desire to remain as independent as I could. This was also the same neurologist that supported my request to not have permanent cauterization surgery.

I continued to adapt and utilized an electric scooter for long distances and embraced the modifications to my van that included the installation of a hydraulic hoist lift that was strong enough to lift my electric scooter. Simply with a push of a button it lowered and lifted my electric scooter from the floor and easily maneuvered and placed it securely in the back trunk of the van. I was in control again. I was mobile and didn't have to rely on others to drive me around. This felt good. No—let me rephrase this—this felt *great* and was one of the most liberating and empowering feelings I had felt in a long time.

I began to use the scooter while attending a junior college that was located on top of a hill. The electric scooter helped tremendously as it was sometimes difficult for me to walk the long distances. The leg braces gave my legs extra support but were heavy and sometimes tired me. The use of the electric scooter meant I had less falling or tripping episodes. When my neurologist said to me, "If you use the electric wheelchair while you are rushing to your classes then you will have more energy left for your family when you get home."

My ongoing evaluations and support from the Department of Rehabilitation resulted in their continued assistance. I am forever grateful to the Department of Rehabilitation for their investment in my educational career goal. In the beginning of this journey, I took only one or two classes per semester. I wanted to test myself and see if I could, in fact, be a student considering my commitments as a mother and my volunteer work at Familia Unida that flourished with more families in need with each year that passed. I was able to manage my personal obligations and career goals thanks to Juan, who modified his work schedule so that he could be available to assist me with the care of the girls or drive me to my evening classes or pick me up so that I would not travel alone in the evenings.

Juan has been the backbone to Familia Unida and why I was able to successfully return to college. It took me several extra years to complete my educational goals along with a decision I made to prolong the classes so that I could adjust my time with family and the ongoing growth of Familia Unida. My husband and daughters were a huge part of my daily assignments that meant many weekend at the university and having playtime with Dad while Mama was in the classroom. The girls would take their roller skates and skateboard and play on the campus, and afterward, we enjoyed our lunch or study time together while their daddy showed them all he could about life's valuable lessons and reiterate to them, and still to this day, *"Pay attention to where you go and know who you are and why you are doing what you do."*

As I learned to manage family, school, and Familia Unida, I decided to dedicate at least one day a week to the multiple sclerosis clinic day at the rehabilitation hospital where I was a patient for over 3 months. I supported the nurses and the clinic doctors with translation and interpreting information that was to be relayed to the patients. Sometimes, I simply shared with the patients how difficult it could be living with an incurable illness. However, my bigger message was about how important it was to communicate their feelings with their loved ones or how urgent it was to seek professional help or reach out to those that loved them if they felt depressed.

During this time was when I also learned that MS was known to cause major depression. I also learned that some of the medications for MS, like the steroids, had a negative side effect of triggering major depression and that a percentage of patients could experience suicidal thoughts. I made it my obligation to inform others about the harsh side effects of steroids and privately told them my personal insight to this. I strongly believe that by my taking steroids, it was one of the contributing factors to the major depression and suicidal thoughts I had experienced a long time ago. The sadness, illness, and disability, along with some medications, can trigger ugly thoughts like I experienced that day by the freeway. It was a horrible, horrible selfish act I do not like to remember. I only reference that day as a reminder to share with someone that may need to hear this reminder. "Be careful when taking medications; read the labels, pay attention to any changes in your mood, and please, reach out for help whenever your gut tells you, you are going through something that doesn't feel right or familiar." Do not go through anything alone. If you are spiritual, call on your faith and pray. Even if you don't believe in God, speak to him or call someone. You will not know how this can improve your situation if you just shut down.

I almost didn't write about that unforgettable day where I was out of control and thought I wanted to leave this earth. I am so glad that I am alive today and found many reasons to live for. Remember, we all count and have a purpose. Ask for support if you don't feel right and let others in when you think that no one will understand. You will see that not everyone is happy all of the time, and for those spurts of gloomy days, let others help bring in sunshine for you and hold on to your faith!

I know now that the lowest day of my life was also the day that I reclaimed my life, and I have chosen life ever since. I want to stress again to those that feel sadness or feel alone sometimes, please take time to understand the side effects of medications and don't discount what the tiny print that describes the side effects have to say. Oftentimes, we think that since the print on the medication is tiny, that means it is not that important. Wrong! Sometimes the writing is small to make it difficult to learn about the poison that can cause bad side effects that are worse than the medical condition that you have. Please surround yourself with those that have compassion and love in their heart. That is already a great step for a healthier you!

I liked volunteering at the rehabilitation facility where I once was a patient. I was happy that the nurses and doctors found my translations in Spanish and interaction with the patients helpful. The medical team had my home telephone number and would call me if they needed my volunteer assistance on a specific day. Donna would contact me from the rehabilitation hospital and refer the Spanish-speaking patients to me to visit or communicate with me directly since at that time there was no information available or accessible in Spanish anywhere in the United States about MS and its effects. Therefore, speaking to someone who was also living with MS, someone that they can talk to in their native tongue, was soothing and a very good start for them.

On one cool day while I was leaving the MS clinic at the rehabilitation center, I passed a man wearing a white lab coat. Our eyes met briefly as I passed him. I was wearing a colorful long summer dress and was wearing my leg braces. We both turned around again, and we both realized that we knew each other. I stopped and looked back again. It was Dr. Saperia, the doctor that had admitted me to the emergency county hospital several years ago. He smiled and said, "Oh my God! It is you! Didn't I tell you that one day you were going to walk again and that we would have our first dance?"

I immediately hugged him with tears in my eyes as I recalled his message of hope. Dr. Saperia spun me around in a circle, right there in the clinic hallway. We pretended to dance to music with similar steps like we were dancing to a waltz. Trust me, my Mexican roots had never given me the experience of dancing a waltz, but in my mind, this is what I felt a waltz would feel like. We both cried with joy, and then shared with the patients and nurses that were around us what had just transpired.

Dr. Saperia said out loud, "I promised Irma a dance when she would walk again!" They clapped as we danced for a few seconds more and watched with curiosity as we reunited. It turned out that he was now the director of the Neurology Department at this facility. We sat down and talked in length about my involvement at the clinic, and he encouraged me to continue to support others who were coping with their illnesses or disabilities. He planted the seed for me to consider conducting support groups at other locations besides my home. Dr. Saperia offered his support and felt strongly that many would benefit from the Spanish-speaking support groups and sharing my message of hope to many more individuals and families.

I continued to volunteer at the MS clinic and met many wonderful patients and made many new friends living with MS who represented various cultures too. I was happy to assist however I could and continued inviting my new MS Spanish-speaking friends to my home. In my living room, I translated the brochures the best I could that were only available in English from the national MS organization. I shared community resources that I had learned about from earlier years from working at the information counter at the State building.

My husband made barbeques in our backyard for our new friends. Sometimes we just laughed or cried and hugged while we reinforced to each other that we were not alone—*no estas solo* is what I said when we ended our visits from our home. Other times, I let them test-drive my scooter in my driveway or on the side the street. We engaged in dialogues that supported them with navigating the many ways that there were to support them that they qualified for, and often, the services and resources were at no cost.

I used to keep the confidential information about my MS friends in my oven. *Why my oven?* The oven burner didn't work. Therefore, we didn't use it, and I rarely baked so this was the perfect place to keep their personal information that I referred to when I would see them again or call them to see how they were coming along. I didn't have an office, desk, or file cabinet so the oven idea I thought was a good private place since it didn't work. Their contact information and my messy notes were kept private in my oven, and no one opened this special safe place but me. By now, there were 20 families that would come over to our home while others stayed in touch by phone too.

"During my darkest moment, faith and family brought peace and a purpose." Simply Love

Chapter 10

Martha Sanchez

$\mathcal{O}$ne late November afternoon I received a phone call from Dr. Saperia. He shared insight about one of his young Latina patients who had inspired him, and he felt strongly that we would be good friends. Her name was Martha Sanchez. She was in her early 20s and had been living with MS since her early teens. Apparently, Martha had just lost her vision a month earlier due to MS complications when I learned about her. Not only had the disease progressed, resulting in paralysis of her upper and lower extremities, Martha was also now dealing with the loss of her eyesight in both of her eyes. Dr. Saperia told me that the loss of her vision had devastated her, and he felt that we would be good for each other.

I immediately felt close to young Martha and her mom after a long phone call of sharing. I already knew that Martha was one of the most amazing young ladies I had ever met in my life just from our initial phone call. Our excitement to meet in person early the following week was mutual. Martha had a gentle and charismatic personality. She had the softest voice that reminded me of young Shirley Temple. She was Mexican, bilingual, and despite her loss of vision, her spirit for life was fascinating. Martha was humble, and she had a mature demeanor that was respected by her mom and siblings with whom she lived. Martha and her family lived approximately 25 minutes from me.

On my drive back home that late afternoon, I couldn't help but compare her physical situation to mine. How scared I was to possibly lose my vision, and here Martha showed me by her example her inner strength and beauty despite the progression that kept her confined to her bed most days, and now...blind. I admired her courage and her loving spirit despite the physical limitations that were apparent. Her faith and family had given her peace and even humor to continue to make the best of this situation.

Martha was confined to her bed most days and used an electric wheelchair with the assistance of her mom. This electric chair had multiple devices that made it easy for her mom to assist her. She appeared comfortable in her wheelchair as her legs and waist were strapped securely with the black Velcro belts that were long and strong. Martha touched the tiny button positioned on her right handrail with her finger. Her petite hands appeared weak and trembled a little when she was attempting to push the button on her electric chair that traveled slowly toward me. Most of her fingers from both hands were twisted in a manner that caused some of her fingers to be pulled back. Her mom was close by a few inches away and ready to offer her assistance if she needed it.

She smiled and said, "This is my old chair and my favorite one." I looked to my right side and barely noticed another wheelchair that had several items neatly stacked on top of it. Despite the ongoing chronic pain and progression of this incurable illness, Martha's happy personality included making sure that her younger twin sisters who were approximately 11 did their homework and that they listened to their mother was on the top of her list of priorities.

I had never in my life met anyone like Martha who, despite the progression of her illness, continued to find humor and kept us laughing. She would say to me, "I have another funny story to tell you, but first I have to let that horrible spasm go through my body so I won't scream in the middle of my funny story, okay?" The painful spasm would last for a few minutes at a time and caused most of her body to twist and turn throughout the duration of the spasm. Then she would take a deep breath and smiled faintly right before the spasm would come and would say, "I hope this spasm is a short one and that the longer ones wait and don't come until after you leave because we have a lot to talk about." Then she said quietly, "I hope my sisters' friends don't come over until after you leave because I like to keep an eye on them." Then she would say, "Get it? I'm going to keep *an eye* on them?"...making a joke about her not being able to actually see them.

Martha could hear everything. She said her hearing had somehow become clearer and she could hear from further away distances than before her vision loss. She was silly and scolded her twin sisters when they didn't do their homework! Despite her current physical limitations, paralysis in most of her body, and her vision loss, she was in charge of the house. Martha was the dominant figure that her sisters respected.

She gave hope and inspiration to everyone that came in contact with her, reminding her sisters that without an education they wouldn't find a good job and informed them that they had to stay in school and not miss any more days. Martha did all of this—mostly from her bed. From her soft-spoken energized voice she demonstrated so much love for life and her family and now our friendship became stronger. I grew to love her more. I learned from Martha about the importance of doing what you love to do and to follow your passion no matter what.

Martha, in her early 20s, counseled her mom who was a religious person and often cried out of frustration and sadness because of her daughter's pain or mobility limitations. Martha's mom spoke only Spanish and was the caregiver to her 3 daughters. I liked to sing and read to Martha because she said that helped her to escape from her pain. She also liked to listen to music and especially loved a Spanish musical group that sang lyrics to profound messages related to social justice with a rhythm that made her move around like she was dancing from her bed or from her electric wheelchair. Martha liked it when my daughters braided her beautiful long hair and gave her updates from what they did that afternoon or while at school.

As a family, we offered our friendship and support to our new friends. What was disturbing to witness was that even though Martha spoke both English and Spanish, she no longer could translate or read the materials about MS that were made available in English only because now she could not read them due to her recent blindness and because her mother could not read English. Therefore, a huge void existed of helplessness and disconnect for her mother and others that I was able to meet.

Martha's family situation was not an isolated incident. I became aware of other families who did not read or write in English and were confused about their medical condition due to language and cultural barriers. Martha's blindness added to the disconnect to available resources and support from mainstream MS organizations that had critical important updates related to new developments and treatment options that were soon going to be available.

Martha and I had many dialogues about how we would bring the Latino or Spanish-speaking MS community together so they wouldn't live with this alone or feel isolated. We would implement many more ideas once she felt stronger. She eagerly anticipated going to my home soon to meet our Familia Unida members in person that I told her about that came to visit me at my home to gather for counsel, sharing of resources, or simply for a hug or a cry together. Martha would express to me, "Soon I will also go to your house, but not yet because I still have many more doctor appointments." Sometimes her speech was slurred and that frustrated her as she had so much that she wanted to share.

I told her that soon we would unite many more families and when her condition stabilized she would meet them and they would be inspired by her as she had inspired me and all who come in contact with her. Martha smiled and replied, "Remind me to take my favorite music so that we can dance with them too, okay?" I replied, "Yes, that's a great idea."

"It didn't matter what we looked like, what mattered was the passion and love we shared for life." Simply Love

Chapter 11

My Salvation

After my diagnosis of multiple sclerosis, I wanted to learn as much as I could about MS, treatment options, and resources available. I especially wanted to be connected to others who were also living with this medical condition. I felt a sense of relief to learn that there was a place to go to. I became involved with the largest MS organization in the United States and dedicated my time to participate in their fundraisers to raise awareness and support for further research in hopes of finding a cure.

This MS organization had been in existence for 50 years at the time. I participated in the MS walk held nearby at the beach in Santa Monica. I enjoyed being a volunteer at the MS booth and gave out English materials about this organization. I encouraged others to donate and support this MS organization to find a cure. With my family, we brought awareness of this organization to the community. I was thrilled that my sister Jackie participated in the MS Bike-athon fundraiser on my behalf. She rode her bike with other strangers who came together for the common goal of supporting someone they loved. We collected donations for this great cause. I helped out in their MS registration booth and provided materials in English about MS.

On another occasion, I was excited because, together with the support of my family and friends, we raised over $1,500 in donation pledges for this MS organization.

My family and friends named our walk group "Familia Unida" (United Family) and our group of approximately 12 walked besides me while I traveled in my teal blue scooter during the MS walk hosted at Griffith Park. We held signs that we made to show support. One said, "FAMILIA UNIDA SUPPORTS MS." My young daughters, now 9 and 10 years old, held signs that they made with colorful markers that read messages of love and support "CURE MS" and "I SUPPORT MY MAMA." I applauded this organization for their national presence and commitment to finding a cure for multiple sclerosis in the United States. It was a great feeling to stroll in my electric scooter along side my family and close friends that held signs they had made. The photos captured that day take me back to a time of uncertainty and longing for hope for a cure.

My first experience in living with MS and witnessing that the Spanish-speaking MS community was disconnected from this established MS organizations didn't make sense to me. Yes, I became knowledgeable of treatment options, available resources, and critical research updates related to upcoming treatment options. However, I was meeting Spanish speaking only MS friends who were not benefiting from this invaluable resource and support. It became my personal commitment to bring awareness to the many families of color who I was meeting and who I knew would benefit from the MS research updates and this huge MS organization. I echoed this sentiment to the big MS organization as soon as I found out how many more Spanish speaking MS patients would contact me for support. Initially and immediately, I pleaded that I could help and be the link to those I was meeting at the hospital and clinics who did not know about them.

I did not plan to create a nonprofit organization to bring awareness to the Spanish-speaking MS community. I knew nothing about running a nonprofit. This term was unfamiliar to me. All I knew was that many people were not able to make that connection with them because unfortunately, at the time there were no materials or services available in Spanish. Therefore, there was a disconnect and confusion expressed amongst many of the Spanish speaking community who expressed that they felt alone and unsure as to what was happening to them now that they were given this diagnosis of MS. Keep in mind that the only information available or accessible at that time was in English and there was no internet, email, text yet available or the worldwide web. Treatment medications were barely being discussed and would come in the future. I began to notice other barriers that were evident when poverty and isolation from mainstream resources were nonexistent when language and cultures and lack of awareness of available resources are not reaching certain groups or populations.

During my earlier years of being diagnosed with MS, I saw that the Spanish-speaking MS community was missing from the large MS organization fundraising events where I volunteered. I wanted to do more and bridge the two cultures and bring everyone that needed help together so that all who was dealing with this disease knew where to go and how to heal or get connected. I wanted to implement programs and services in Spanish for those I was meeting that didn't speak English or preferred to gather and have dialogues in their native language. While I participated at the MS Research updates with my husband in the early 1990's somewhere in a large hotel in Downtown Los Angeles or in the Westside of Los Angeles, I noticed that my family and I, and possibly two other brown faces, were the only Latino or Mexicans present at this huge community gathering. I found it a mystery to learn that there was a lack of representation of the Spanish-speaking community. At first, I truly believed that I was possibly the only Mexican living with MS in Southern California. At another large lecture I finally saw another brown face and with excitement went up to introduce myself—only to learn that the nice woman I went to greet smiled and shared that she from India.

I began to wonder why there was a dearth of Mexicans or Latinos sharing in the community meetings and resources regarding this diagnosis. It became my priority to do something about this, and I truly believe that everything happened for a reason, so with the support of family, neighbors, and community leaders, Familia Unida Living with MS was born. Our service model at Familia Unida, which is still true today, is to begin services where the member wants to start. In order words, listening to what they felt they needed assistance with based on their priorities.

Our core principle includes: "All people living with MS desire to be connected and merit equal access." Our motto: "*No Estas Solo*" (You Are Not Alone) remains true today. In this journey living with MS I learned that MS does not discriminate against anyone, and therefore, it is imperative that our service model embraces different cultures, different ethnic backgrounds, and the diverse populations who must live with MS, and also others who are living with different disabilities. We are still considered a grassroots nonprofit organization and have many more years to build the capacity and raise awareness to our commitment to serve many who are counting on us.

In the mid-1990s, as a volunteer and commitment also from my husband and young daughters, we began to host the support group meetings in my living room for approximately 20 families, which kept me busy. I met individuals who were "Spanish speaking only" and expressed similar sentiments about their discontentment when they tried reaching out for help. They expressed that others would either hang up on them if they spoke in Spanish or apologize and say, "Please have someone else call on your behalf that speaks English because we do not have anyone here who speaks Spanish." These similar sentiments were echoed by others. And other people were just plain rude to them.

In an effort to help, I initially met with the key staff at the large MS organization based in California. I offered to be a volunteer and start a support group meeting in Spanish for the Spanish-speaking MS families. I wanted so desperately to volunteer and work with them at this capacity and not simply raise money to send to the organizations for research. I felt strongly that the urgency right now for many MS patients was to simply understand what was happening to their body and help them get relief from their depression so that they could come out of their sadness and fear. Yes, a cure is what we all wanted, but many people needed help *now* to understand about and learn how to cope so that they could maximize upon their quality of life. They needed help now. It was truly urgent that they receive it now because their fear kept many afraid to even think of the future.

I wanted to bridge the gap between the families I had met that were not getting assistance or support despite their effort to reach out. I left my résumé with the MS organization administration that had been in existence for over 50 years—twice. I also shared in person with their representatives my desire to serve them and my community while highlighting my past skills and experience that referenced my work at a children's orthopedic hospital and my previous employment of working with the government and my support for an elected official. I told of my employment where I greeted the public when people walked into the State building. I had to be knowledgeable enough to inform the guests that entered the State building about the government, community, and county resources. I knew where to go when a person needed free legal advice, government assistance, and a variety of social services. I was the one-stop information person for the county of Los Angeles while I worked for the State of California.

I stressed to this particular, large MS organization that I saw a great need for families who were Spanish speaking and I saw firsthand that they were not being connected to the various MS updates about new medication coming soon or the current MS research or news about upcoming possible treatment options. I made several attempts to offer my volunteer service but was repeatedly told that ". . . unfortunately, at this time we do not have a budget t to support groups in Spanish, nor do we have materials printed in Spanish at this time."

In one final attempt, I called back to share that I was taking their English materials with me to the MS clinic at the rehabilitation center where I volunteered and was also an outpatient. I told them in desperation that I was translating their materials to the best of my ability into Spanish. I shared that I wasn't familiar with some of the medical terminology and I wanted to ensure that I was giving out the correct information that they had sent me in English. I asked again, "Please, could you please translate this important information in Spanish?" The answer again: "I am sorry, but we do not have a budget for that at this time." I asked if they could possibly make me some business cards or provide me with a document confirming that it was okay for me to share their English MS materials and talk about what I had learned from their English brochures. They shared that they could not do that but would be happy to ship me another big box of materials to my home again in English. I was reassured that I had permission to share and translate like I had been doing.

I lost my patience and became frustrated and despondent by their reaction. I found it hard to believe that a support group in Spanish was not important enough for those that preferred to read in Spanish or did not speak English and could only guess what was happening to them now that they were living with a scary illness they knew little about. I say *scary* because when a person is not informed or doesn't understand the changes transpiring in his or her body, it's easy to think the worst— to shut down and give up. I offered my time and support as a 100 percent volunteer—and again, I was told that ". . . someone would call me back about possibly becoming a volunteer at the MS organization." The last person who I spoke to on the phone simply said, "They should all just learn English like you did, don't you think?"

I tearfully shared this news with my husband. I did not know what else I could do. I was only one person and with him, well, we were two. I expressed to him how unfair this was. I thought of my past efforts to support this organization by raising donations for their bike-athon or walkathon and helping out in the registration booth while my sister supported the cause to find a cure.

I was grateful that I was able to understand both languages, but not all people did. Juan looked at me and said, "Why don't you go to the office supply store?" He recalled that I would be able to purchase 1,000 business cards made for only $9.99. Juan said that I could put our home telephone number and include my name on the card, and this way, I could give them out at the MS clinic and the other places that were calling me and where I visited so they would at least have a card to call me so I could continue to tell them what I was learning about MS. I liked that idea and responded, "I would also leave some with the various doctors and different clinics." All the resources and support that I knew about were free, or cost little. Besides, the information that I was sharing was not costing me anything, simply my time and the expense of a higher phone bill.

I was excited when Juan echoed my sentiments and said, "You are correct. It's not costing us anything to share resources. He reminded me of my previous employment that included giving out information and connecting folks that came to the State of California information counter where I worked before and became knowledgeable about community resources and government programs from all levels of city, county, state, and federal governments.

A few days later, Juan took me to the office supply store and paid for the cards that included the name Familia Unida Living with MS and my home telephone number and contact information on them. Together, including our daughters, we continued to provide whatever we could from our home. We agreed that sharing love and linkage to resources was easy to do, so we made it our priority to offer support however we could.

I liked the name Familia Unida (United Family) because it symbolized that we were the family to many new friends who became our extended family, and we were united as a family through the connection of MS that reminded us: "You Are Not Alone" (*No Estas Solo*). Together, we would find support and be strong like a united family. For others they expressed that we had become their family and bonds were established and support continued to flourish in many neighborhoods, especially in the low-income pockets of Los Angeles and cities throughout Southern California. Caucasians, Filipinos, and blacks would also call us and say, "Hi, Irma, I have MS, and I was given your card at the clinic, but I am not Latino. May I join your group?" I would reply with the same sentiment, "Of course, Familia Unida is for anyone who wishes to be a member." The next question was, "Do I have to pay to be a member?"

The response was always the same: "There is no fee for membership. Being a member of Familia Unida simply means that you chose to be a part of Familia Unida and that you can be a part of our family for as long as you wish.". Some asked if I belong to Familia Unida can I also be a part of the other big MS organization? Our response was always the same, maximize your resources and support and benefit from all places that can help you.

Familia Unida was officially born in our living room in the mid-1990s. We hosted the first public meeting at the Rosemead Community Center in January of 1998. We welcomed the established MS organization that had been around for over 50 years to come and meet many of the MS Spanish-speaking community who were present and had visited at my home before the formal convening in 1998 at the Rosemead Center. I wanted them to see the rainbow of faces and cultures, and especially the Latino Community that also merited their attention. They asked me if they could take a photo to showcase the Latino community living with MS who I had been supporting from my home or over the phone for years. I responded, "If it's okay with them, it's okay with me."

In the following month I was surprised to receive the newsletter in my mailbox from the largest MS organization In that had referenced Familia Unida as a group that they started with their group leader Irma Resendez. I was shocked to read the national MS article that stated that I was a group leader for that organization and that Familia Unida was a support group under their umbrella of services. I thought of the countless times that I pleaded to be affiliated with them as a volunteer and how every time they had rejected my volunteer assistance. Hummm..it was because of them that I founded Familia Unida Living with MS in my home years earlier. Their presence that evening at the Rosemead Community Center was because Familia Unida Living with MS had extended an invitation to them so that they could witness the many beautiful brown faces alongside their families that were living with MS and who now had a place to receive support. As a group that evening, we urged them to please provide materials in Spanish.

Familia Unida did not have the resources to print these items. We barely had enough money to keep up with the phone bill. Their newsletter of that special convening captured a beautiful photo of many of the Spanish-speaking members and their families present that evening, It was a blessing that the largest Spanish language media outlets were present that same Friday evening who recognized Familia Unida as the first MS group in the United States to reach out to the Spanish-speaking MS community. The Familia Unida members and my family were thankful to read the articles and news media from the mainstream media outlets that captured the true sentiment of what had really transpired that Friday evening at the Rosemead Community Center in 1998. This was the beginning of a Familia Unida grassroots nonprofit organization that was formed to reinforce that "You Are Not Alone" (*No Estas Solo*).

My ultimate goal that remains true today is that all people merit equal access to serve and support despite language or cultural identities.

Today, I am thrilled to see that this concept of unity is widely accepted and more awareness to address this inequality is ongoing. There is more support available for many. However, there is still room for improvement.

Familia Unida helped to mobilize the larger MS organizations that had the financial stability to make important changes to better serve all who needed support. For example, to develop materials and support in Spanish for those that preferred this or needed it.

A few years ago, I was invited to speak at a National press conference at the California State Capitol to speak about health care and the inequalities and disparities affecting low-income families living with MS and other chronic medical conditions. While in Sacramento, an unexpected surprise occurred. The national MS organization invited me as their guest to attend a dinner that they were hosting at a nearby hotel. I accepted and attended with my daughter Jacqueline who had requested time off from her work to join me on my important trip to Sacramento. This was the first time that I had ever attended one of their dinners.

To our surprise, that night, a representative from the national MS organization at the podium asked me to stand while he publically acknowledged Familia Unida Living with MS for being the first MS organization in the country to reach out to the Spanish-speaking community. This public verbal acknowledgment me also for being selected as the Women of the Year for the State of California nominated by Senator Ed Hernandez, Chair of the Health Committee. I was happy to see my daughter next to me smile with contentment as she witnessed this kind message.

Some have encouraged Familia Unida to have a MS walkathon to support our members, and we think this is a great idea. With more volunteers and experts in this area we will make this a reality in the near future. To this date, the National MS organization has never provided any financial assistance to Familia Unida, and this goes back to our inception as a nonprofit in 1998. It is important to clarify this misconception because some of our new members think that we are the same organization. In earlier years, some of Familia Unida board members hosted a meeting in downtown with the executive director from this large local MS chapter. Our goal was to see how we could compliment each other's goal to serve the MS community and possibly work together. Their sentiment was that they were sorry that they were not able to financially offer assistance and support our nonprofit as they were busy building their nonprofit and did not have a budget to support this grassroots organization. They were nice and encouraged us to continue to refer our clients to them and they provided us with materials that gave insight to their programs, services and fundraising events.

On the other hand, another Multiple Sclerosis organization based in Florida, "Multiple Sclerosis Foundation", Terry Roir contacted me after learning about Familia Unida's grassroots efforts. They were thrilled to find a place that they could refer the Spanish speaking community. They were generous to invite Juan and I to visit their office in Florida and went as far as welcoming us into their home. Thanks to their support, we learned firsthand about their operations and programs and received hands-on insight to running a nonprofit. The Multiple Sclerosis Foundation, "MSF," sponsored the cost of my home phone bill for several years when I served from my home. The MSF had a brand-new desk, computer, and file cabinet shipped to my home. They offered to purchase as many as we needed. However, all I needed at the time was one of each, and that's what we ordered. When we arrived back home to California a few days later, all the items that we picked from the catalog had already arrived to our home.. We transformed one of our bedrooms to a home office thanks to their investment that sponsored our initial real office. The administrator at the MS foundation in Florida and their magnificent team highlighted Familia Unida in their newsletter on several occasions for being the first MS organization in the United States to serve the Spanish-speaking community. Juan and I will always be grateful to the MSF and others who are serving our community with a loving and giving heart, which I believe are the core principles for building strong communities.

Familia Unida continues with our mission and serves as best as possible with a small budget and huge hearts. Our priceless resources have been the beautiful friendships and diverse University and High School internship and volunteer program. We realize now more than ever that we need to match our passion to serve with sufficient financial backing in order to support and assist the many families that keep coming. Our strength is through a dynamic board and our compassionate team, including kind experts, who have collectively made it possible for Familia Unida to provide services to over 15,000 people living with MS as well as services and programs for individuals and families living with various types of disabilities. Adam Melendez, Familia Unida's current Board President and long time supporter has been instrumental with the production of the annual "Wheelchair Wash and Health Access Fair" by providing all the tents and promotional items so that thousands of guest could receive a full day of pampering under a tent and in the shade. His heartfelt private or surprise gifts to families in needs brought happy faces to some who were reminded that someone cared. Its because of the many acts of kindness from friends and strangers alike who share of their heart that have made it possible for Familia Unida to continue to flourish, despite the difficult and financial stressors that are sometimes felt as we serve.

"Sharing love is priceless, and it doesn't matter if you are rich or poor. Anyone can give this gift, and everyone deserves it." Simply Amor

Chapter 12

MS *Familia Unida*

$\mathcal{T}$he founding of Familia Unida was my personal salvation that brought healing and defined my purpose in life. I have learned how to really live my life and to let go of the many stressors that were insignificant prior to my diagnosis of MS. Every morning that I could wake up, feel my heartbeat, breathe, think, talk, and walk reminded me that I had another opportunity to make today a beautiful day. Since my diagnosis and after my lowest point of my life was also when I vowed to serve God and have him present in my daily routine. From the moment that I head out in traffic, I thank God for the opportunity to listen to my favorite music while I drive in traffic. When someone cuts me off on the highway, I pray for that driver that he finds peace and calms down. When the angry person complained about the long line at the market, I smile and share a positive message so she or he is distracted for a brief moment and forgets about the long line.

In my new life with living with multiple sclerosis for over 21 years now, I have witnessed how easily a life can be taken away or changed for the worst in a few seconds from an accident, illness, disability, tragedy, or crisis, and it is now a part of your new reality. These uncomfortable and sometime painful experiences reminded me that I didn't feel the same and others may not treat me the same either. Yes, once illness, disability, and even depression are now a part of you, they can eat up your soul, spirit, and the desire to live. I know that life has no guarantees for anyone. Therefore, I have learned an important lesson: Why wait until tragedy or the unexpected hits home to begin celebrating you and those you care about?

Don't wait until you are desperate to do all that you wish to do, because an illness or horrible experience can change all that. Celebrate and find ways to fulfill your passion now and not simply because now you have received bad news and your time on earth has suddenly been shortened. Be among the walking living and not the walking dead that lack the spirit or motivation to accept happiness. Do it now! No more excuses for not having a lovely day. Start smiling for waking up to the delicious smell of coffee or to your little ones giggling in the hallway or for enjoying your pet that is there for you whenever you are alone.

In many ways, given this diagnosis of multiple sclerosis many years ago was a blessing because it helped me to see very clearly what was important, which prompted me to dedicate my life doing only what I like to do and sharing my positive energy with anyone that crosses my path. We do not know when our last day on earth will be...our last hour or last minute or last second. Make your mornings, afternoons, and evenings the most peaceful and loving experience of your life! If you are blessed to wake up the next morning, appreciate the beauty and blessings that are all around you. Keep on living with excitement and feel love all over again and again and greatness will follow. Feel love and you will have more to share.

"Love is endless, and every day is a new beginning." Simply Amor

Chapter 13

Mexico Smiles ~ International Debut

$\mathcal{I}$n the 1990s during the Christmas holidays, I received the first call from one of the mainstream Spanish language television news stations. They were interested in covering a story about Familia Unida and meeting some of the families served. The media crew came to my home initially to begin the interview. Soon thereafter, the media crew followed me in their van and we traveled to one of our members' home that desperately wanted to share a message to the world about the urgent need to find a cure for MS because her daughter in her early 20s was painfully dying and she did not know how to help her other than through prayer. Seeing our member confined to her bed and in a deep sleep because she had just taken the pain medication gave me a sense of peace to know that at that moment, she was not screaming from the spasms that painfully traveled her body and brought tears to her, and especially her mother.

The Spanish language news reporter appeared almost shocked to see the young beautiful girl laid in silence. He noticed her hands and fingers were permanently twisted while her mom tearfully shared that MS had taken her daughter's vision and had paralyzed most of her body.

She informed us that when the first symptoms began to appear, she was in junior high school. It progressed when she was a cheerleader in high school. She expressed how she carried her *mija* in her arms to bathe her in the tub and with pride talked about her younger daughters who helped too as best as they could to make their sibling as comfortable as possible in her surroundings.

Her room was filled with photos of family and friends, music cassettes, earphones, bright stuffed animals, medical appliances, bed liners, folded clothing, and sheets that were neatly placed by her bed. The mama cried as she expressed that it was difficult to watch her firstborn deteriorate right before her eyes. I acknowledged in Spanish during the live interview that more help and treatment options were necessary for the Latino community so that this young girl and people suffering with MS could get better assistance and support.

The news reporter recognized Familia Unida for taking the first steps in bringing awareness to the Latino MS community and ended the interview by asking me, "Where should a person call should they wish to contact you or find out more about Familia Unida Viviendo con Esclerosis Múltiple (the Spanish translation of Familia Unida Living with MS)?" I provided him with my home telephone number, as that was the only telephone line that I had. Familia Unida provided emotional support and a platform for a member's mother to voice her agonizing reality that had taken her daughter's health to a rapidly destructive state at such a young age. This was during a time period that there were yet no treatment medications available to slow down the progression of MS. She was one of many families who expressed similar sentiments while living in isolation or fear prior to connecting with Familia Unida. Now, she, like others, no longer had to feel like they were the only one dealing with this new way of life. Her daughter continued to lay in a deep sleep and was unaware of our presence as her mother asked for urgent help to cure her daughter. It was a plea from a mother in deep anguish. She said that God had heard her prayers as she could finally share her sentiments to a reporter that would capture her testimony and share what her daughter has painfully been experiencing for many years.

Sharing my home phone number with the media resulted in more families contacting me at my home. More and more Spanish-speaking individuals called, asking for assistance for their spouse or child who was recently diagnosed or who had been living with MS for many years without ever talking to another person in Spanish about their medical condition.

Following the increase in calls, the largest Spanish newspaper conducted an interview with me and also interviewed several of the members who shared their frustration or despair regarding how long they had attempted to obtain support or referrals to services without success until connecting with Familia Unida. I became concerned that the ongoing calls that came at all hours of the day and night would not stop. This made me sad because I had no idea that there were so many others suffering or living in silence with this disease. I was naïve to think that there were only 20 or more Latino families that were living with MS.

One late afternoon I received a call from Dr. Saperia who wanted to let me know that Martha had returned again to the intensive care unit and that he was not sure if she would make it this time. It was raining hard that day. I decided to go soon after speaking with him. Juan said he would stay home with the girls and asked that I travel by street since he felt that was the best route given the current weather.

By this time, our daughters had grown to love Martha. They would take turns sharing stories with her or braiding her hair while we gathered around her bed. Other times we just sat around her bed and listened to music or heard about her weekly updates that primarily revolved around her sisters who were now preteens. Martha would share in frustration that her younger sisters were beginning to show signs of testing her and her ability to make them accountable for their homework and other chores that her mom needed help with. Nevertheless, her sisters adored her, and it was beautiful to witness the family listen to the young leader's words of wisdom. Martha had earned their respect and love. It didn't matter that she no longer could see them or that she communicated from her bed. What mattered to Martha was that her younger sisters did well in school. She made it her responsibility to share important life lessons with them in hopes of preparing them for their future.

When my daughter Jacqueline heard that I was going to visit Martha that rainy evening after Dr. Saperia's phone call, she immediately expressed, "Mama, I don't want to see Martha at that hospital." She was referring to that hospital where her mama lived for several months years ago. I agreed, and I did not have any intention of taking my daughters with me to that visit. I found it very interesting that at the young age of now 11 years old she was able to verbalize what she felt and spoke up about whatever it was she had on her mind.

Johnnie, on the other hand, said, "Mama, I want to go with you to visit Martha." I discouraged her by telling her that she was in the intensive care unit and that she probably wouldn't recognize us this time. I expressed that her doctor had said that she was now in a coma. Johnnie became serious. She said, "Please, Mama, I want to see Martha one last time." I tried to discourage Johnnie by sharing that when a person was in a coma they were not able to speak and that it would be like she was resting and asleep. I added that Martha was now on life support, which meant that she was kept alive by a breathing machine and that she was no longer breathing on her own. I told her that it would be best that she remember Martha as she did when she visited her at her home. Johnnie pulled my hand as I was leaving and said one last time, "Please, Mama, I want to say good-bye." I looked at my husband and made the decision at that moment to allow Johnnie to go with me. I told her that if she changed her mind on the way over there that that would be okay and that Martha would know that she was close by.

I took my time driving to the hospital as it started to rain harder. I told myself that I shouldn't have taken Johnnie out of the house under this horrible weather condition. I prayed and asked God to get us there safely and to give us strength and to fill Martha with peace as I drove in silence.

When we arrived, Johnnie let me know by her body language that she was going in with me. Martha was alone, the room was dark, she lay beautiful with her eyes closed surrounded by plastic tubes that were connected to her. The breathing machine was pumping loudly as her body was forced to breathe in and out. Martha was not aware that we were there. Or was she? I pondered this question as I recalled when I was at the county hospital and heard everything my family was saying in their whispers over my bed years ago when they thought I was in a deep sleep.

I took a deep breath and tried to control my emotions. I knew that this time would be the last time I would see her. I thought I was prepared, but I wasn't even close. I privately prayed over Martha. In my private thoughts I thanked her for being courageous and showing me her happiness. I asked her how she did that. So happy and full of life. She was the happiest person I had ever met in my life even though she endured so much pain all day long. I thanked her for showing me that there was only time for happy moments and that I would remember her every time I felt like giving up.

Martha and I had shared the vision of bringing awareness to the many voices that needed medical attention. I held on to Johnnie's hand without saying a word. She was also in tears. I said, "Martha is resting now and without pain." Johnnie's innocence and love for Martha was transparent. We left after a few minutes.

It continued to rain as we traveled on the street back home. Johnnie sat quietly in the front seat, and I also drove in silence. As I reached the stoplight I looked at her. Johnnie had her face turned completely away, facing her window while I drove back home in the rain. She was trying to hide from me that she was crying in silence. Her tears continued to roll down her cheek. I squeezed her hand tightly and whispered to her, "*Mija*, this is why I didn't want to take you to visit Martha. I knew that this would be very painful for you." She looked right at me in a composed and mature manner at age 12 and tearfully responded, "This is not why I am crying, Mama. I am crying because if we didn't go visit Martha, who would?"

At that moment, I got chills up and down my entire body and the hairs on my arms stood up. I was not expecting that kind of response. She conveyed to me that she felt a personal obligation to be there for her, reinforcing our previous communication: "You Are Not Alone" (*No Estas Solo*). Johnnie knew, at that young age, why I did what I did. She had matured beyond her years right in front of me.

We both cried out loud, laughed, and reflected on the many gifts of courage and support Martha gave to her family and her friends. We were thankful to know that she loved us as we loved her and agreed that it was a good thing that we went together to visit Martha.

A few days had passed when I received a call very early in the morning. It must have been around 5:45 a.m. A man identified himself as Marcos, an older gentleman possibly in his late sixties. He was speaking rather loudly and rapidly in Spanish. He asked, "Is this Irma Resendez?" I said "*Sí*" (yes). He began to speak louder and faster in Spanish. He thanked me for bringing attention to MS and those that only spoke Spanish. He said that his wife Rebecca was Puerto Rican and they were excited to talk with me because they thought that his wife was the only Spanish-speaking person living with MS because her doctor didn't know of any other patients with this diagnosis of esclerosis múltiple (MS). He expressed their relief to finally be able to hear about another person living with MS that also spoke Spanish.

When he read about what Familia Unida was doing, he had to connect with me and also wanted me to speak with his wife who was waiting by the phone. With excitement I told him, "Yes, I can hear her in the background!" She was yelling out loud, in Spanish, "*Si es ella? Es la Sra. Resendez?*" (Is it her? Is it Mrs. Resendez?) In Spanish I could now hear her voice louder than her husband's as she yelled out to him, "Give me the phone. I want to speak to Sra. Irma. Give me the phone," she said again to him.

The Spanish-speaking lady identified herself as Rebecca. She said that she wanted to meet me in person and talk to me about what she had experienced all these years. I asked her in Spanish how long had she been living with MS. She tearfully cried, "Since 1975." I replied, "What?" I was in total disbelief. *1975?* She said, "Yes, all these years I have prayed to meet someone that understood what I was feeling." She gave thanks to God that she had found me. She became very emotional and cried and laughed and said again that she wanted me to go to her home where I could spend a day or as long as I liked so that we could share our experiences. I cried with joy that we were going to meet. It made me sad to know that for over 25 years she had never talked to or met anyone living with MS. She shared how awful it was to know that there was no medication for this and sometimes the pain was ugly and unbearable. She started to cry when she shared that her memory would get confused sometimes and her walking was limited.

This older woman in her late sixties said that she used a wheelchair most days but that sometimes she used a cane. What she felt the worst about was the depression that would creep up and keep her in bed a lot. She shared how she would tell her husband to go away so that she could disappear because she didn't have anything to offer him anymore. Then her tears turned to laughter as she said, "*Pero mi viejo no se quiere ir*" ("But my old man refuses to leave"). She asked if she could be a part of Familia Unida. I responded, "Absolutely!"

I rushed to get a piece of paper so that I could write down her address and her telephone number so that I could go meet her in person soon. I started to write the name of the street on my notebook, where I kept all of the numbers and names of my new MS familia. The street that I wrote down did not sound familiar to me and all the words were in Spanish. Then I began to write down the city and that was also unfamiliar. When she shouted out that she lived in Puerto Rico, I said, "What? *Puerto Rico?* You are so far from me. Your husband said you were Puerto Rican, but I didn't realize you were in Puerto Rico. You sound so close." I told her that I was in California and that I could not go to Puerto Rico. I said, "It's only my family and I who are sharing resources, and we live in Rosemead, California." I told her that sometimes we go visit those that live close by in the city of Los Angeles.

Then I asked her, "How did you get my phone number?" She responded, "Yes, I know you are in California. I saw a photo of you and read your story." "Where?" She responded, "From the local newspaper." She mentioned the name of the newspaper, but I was unaware of that newspaper. I was very confused. I expressed that I was so happy that we had connected. I apologized when I told her that I was too far away and did not have the money to travel to her. We continued our conversation for almost 25 minutes. We exchanged addresses and would continue to stay in touch and would also take turns calling each other. Before ending the call, she said again that I was welcomed anytime to visit her and that her humble home was my home! *"Mi casa es su casa."* What a very nice woman. I wished that I could miraculously have her over for breakfast and have long conversations instead of our rapid talking because we were both sensitive to the call being long distance. She seemed, like me, to have limited financial resources. I knew though that we would continue to have meaningful conversations. I thanked her again. She had made my day is what I told her. She said if she had the money she would pay for me to go stay with her and meet in person. I told her that we could pretend that she was down the street because her call was so clear and it did feel like she was close by. We laughed and agreed that I would call her periodically and she agreed that she would do the same. Despite the distance we were now connected and thanked God for bringing us together. I said that the next call would be me calling her but that it would be on a weekend when the cost was cheaper. These were some of the many faces that I never saw, but I felt their smiles as we communicated during the long-distance calls.

A few hours after that call, I received another call from a woman named Maria who said she was calling me from Mexico City! She was delighted to finally talk to someone else that was living with MS. It was exhilarating to speak with someone from so far away and feel a connection. I shared that I had visited Mexico City and that my father was born at the D.F., the state capitol from where she was calling me. She said, "Who knows, maybe we are family"—a thought that I was about to say too! I wished that I could invite these wonderful new friends into my living room so that we could hug and simply converse and learn about each other and see how I could offer support or services or whatever I could. Like the woman who I spoke too earlier that day, she had a similar response, "I got your phone number from my local Spanish language newspaper." Again, it was a name that I was not familiar with.

I began to panic and got excited at the same time. I realized that somehow my home telephone number was mentioned in newspapers in various places in various states and countries. What was impressionable was to speak with great people who represented various parts of the world and how through this illness called MS we immediately connected in a way like if we were a part of a fraternity or a family that would be there for each other simply because of the diagnosis of MS. This incident reminded me of the name that I selected to represent us. "Familia Unida" (United Family). We were like a family, a family that would be united regardless of where we lived.

Soon after that call, I called the reporter from my favorite Spanish language newspaper in California who had interviewed me. The reporter answered and I said, "José, it's Irma Resendez." I'm certain that he could feel the excitement and worry in my voice as I began to share that I had received several calls that day from seven Spanish-speaking individuals living with MS. Now I was the one talking fast, like those that had called earlier with excitement in their voices. I said, "One was calling me from Puerto Rico and another person called from Mexico City! Others called from Northern California and some called from Los

Angeles." I asked him, "How did that happen? Some said that they read about it from newspapers that I had never heard about."

He laughed with contentment and said "Felicidades! (Congratulations!) Many newspapers picked up the story!" He continued, "Familia Unida was the first MS group in the United States and possibly in other countries, bringing attention to the Spanish-speaking MS community."

I responded, "José, I am not able to serve families in different states, and for sure, not in other countries. How would I do this? Do we need to somehow tell the newspapers to mention that? Can you tell them that we are in California?"

He laughed louder and said, "The news is already out. Don't worry; more articles will be written, and you can say whatever you think needs to be said." He reminded me that the article did say I was in California. He tried to reassure me that this was good news. He said, "Remember, you wanted to bring awareness and support to Latinos living with MS, and, well, it's happening!"

I was serious while all along he was laughing and he expressed he felt somewhat accomplished because people were responding and talking about the story that he had written. I asked him, "How did other newspapers in other countries write a story about Familia Unida?" I was shocked. I asked him, "Could you please stop this? I don't know how to help people living elsewhere." For sure I was not able to help people in other countries. I said, "I was hoping that we might be able to possibly reach just maybe 10 more families in Los Angeles."

He laughed again and said, there was no way to stop the newspaper from running the articles. It already ran. He took time to explain the process of news and how other newspapers could pick it up and that it went through a worldwide wire network where some read and some would call. He got serious and told me that I should not be surprised if more people called.

Even though I was so far from other states and countries it felt good that awareness about the Spanish-speaking community living with MS was now being talked about and this was a new beginning. I prayed that doctors and those in power who could help the afflicted in those cities and countries would indeed help them.

Despite my excitement to speak and possibly meet some really nice people from various parts of the city of Los Angeles, in the United States, and even from Mexico and other countries, I was concerned. I knew that José was right and that more calls would follow. My resources and support groups were limited to the county of Los Angeles and support group meetings hosted in my living room. What was I thinking? The Spanish language nationally known newspaper had included my home telephone number as I had given them permission to do so. My immediate thought was sadness. I had no idea that there were so many others who thought that they were the only ones living with MS. I wished that I could help them or tell them that there was somewhere or someone closer to them in their state or city or country that could help them. But they had already told me that there was nothing available in their vicinity, and that they had tried for years to get help.

I felt overwhelmed and concerned to know that so many had been dealing with MS without support other than with their family, and oftentimes the family felt helpless because they didn't know how to help them. I thought of the nice couple that had been living with MS for over 25 years and never speaking in Spanish to another person who was also living with MS until now.

This was heartbreaking news to me. I knew that I was only one person, and naturally, my family went with me to do home visits in the surrounding cities when Juan was off of work in construction, but even his time was limited. Yes, we had great neighbors who joined to transport the food pantry, but how was I to really be able to help them? I did not have money, didn't have yet an office or printed materials, and could barely pay for the phone bill and gas mileage cost that was more than we had expected or had budgeted for. My oven was still not fixed either. We had to choose between: do we pay for the phone bill or buy groceries for another barbeque for our MS Familia Unida new members who were planning on coming over tomorrow for the first time?

I now knew that there were many more people who were going to learn about Familia Unida. What about them? A part of me was thrilled to know that I had experienced speaking with others in Spanish about MS and I would have never thought that there were people all over the world who also wanted us to bring awareness to them and feel a part of a group where they belonged. I tried to be positive and tell myself that even though we were so far apart from each other, this was a beginning of new dialogues and friendships being built.

I had no idea until that point that there were many more Latino families experiencing similar concerns and who longed, like me, to feel connected. I prayed that soon this would change and that somehow they would finally get the support and medication they were lacking. Hopefully this awareness would lead to more attention and support by the medical community and caring folks in the community who had financial wealth to support more research. A cure and support for Latinos and awareness to the cultural implications living with MS was absolutely necessary.

I now wondered about how many more Spanish-speaking people living with MS were out there that didn't read the article. I wondered about people who spoke other languages or who were of different cultures and backgrounds that also desired assistance and longed to be connected.

I had just walked back in to my home after being outside on my front porch when I received a call from Martha's mom. She wanted to share sad news and let me know that Martha had just passed away less than a half hour ago. This news I knew was coming, but I had tried to convince myself that possibly she would come out of the serious progression again like before. It made me sad to know that I would not be seeing her again. My friend was gone. Martha's mom shared words of gratitude and said over and over again that we had a special bond.

As soon as I hung up the phone Dr. Saperia called. We both felt inspired by her and agreed that at least now she was no longer suffering.

I was not prepared to deal with the news about Martha's passing. I would miss her, and I would never forget her. It was disturbing to know that such a young life, a beautiful spirit who had so many plans to help others despite her chronic condition, was now gone. Shortly after feeling sad I smiled and remembered that I should not be sad. Yes, I would miss her. My faith reminded me that we would all leave this earth eventually and we would go when it is was the exact perfect time... Something we couldn't predict or know for sure. God would also call me when it was my time to go. I told myself that I must continue on my journey to serve as best as I could and as long as I could. I asked for God's blessings, as this was not an easy path. I would leave it at that and gave thanks for the many spiritual gifts that Martha gave me for as long as she was supposed to. I would celebrate her life and the special time that we had together. The profound impact that she made in my life I would remember. Martha was not gone. I could still hear her silly cute voice that had no worries whenever I wanted to.

I called my husband and my daughters to the living room so that I could share the news that I had just received. Silence followed, and tears were shared. Another call came in, and this time from a Spanish-speaking woman living with MS who lived in Florida. She wanted to learn more about Familia Unida and wondered if we would be starting something in her city. I thanked her for calling and reaching out to Familia Unida. Sentiments like those shared by others that lived far away were exchanged. I expressed that, unfortunately, we were only hosting support groups in Los Angeles at the moment but wanted to stay in touch with her and see how else I could assist her. I took down her number and thanked her and shared that I would be calling her next week.

I went back to my family who were still mourning the loss of Martha. I began to question if I could really help others in Martha's memory and honor, and I knew I must. But I didn't know how to do a lot of things.

I interrupted my husband and daughters who were sitting quietly in the living room. I could tell that the talking had just stopped as they waited for me to return. I shared that I could not continue with Familia Unida. I expressed that another person from Florida needs help and lives alone and that I told her that I would call her back next week to discuss more information. I asked my family, "How can we support her?" I tearfully said to them, "It's too hard. There are too many families, and not just here in Los Angeles but all over the world. How am I going to help them?" We had no money or budget for returning the long-distance calls. Everything we did over the last 7 or 8 years was done from our heart and compassion to make a difference and without any financial support other than my Social Security checks that I had earned from working over 10 years prior to my diagnosis. How could we continue with just our passion? Familia Unida needed much more support to sustain the many capacity-building efforts needed.

Besides, Martha was gone, and it was her and my dream to do this together. I advocated for Martha and her family who struggled to understand the English updates about MS that she used to receive in English and used to read to her family before she became blind. I gave insight to this family. Some Latino families speak English but many parents or family members felt more comfortable reading in Spanish, their native language.

I had shared with the community at large, especially the local MS English-speaking community that there were families who didn't speak English or couldn't see and that kept them in isolation from important MS and medical updates because of the language and cultural barriers. I advocated for Martha because since the loss of her eyesight she could no longer read the materials to her mom who only spoke Spanish. But now Martha was gone, and her mother didn't need to read about MS anymore. Martha was truly gone.

I questioned what I had started. How could we possibly think we could make a difference? There was so much I didn't know how to do. While I sat deep in my thoughts, my youngest daughter, Jacqueline, stood in front of me and said, "Mom, what about all the other Marthas out there? We can't stop now. Who is going to help them?" I was shocked to hear Jacqueline, barely 11 years old, scolding me and questioning how could I ever think of giving up when there were so many people that needed us? I looked at Johnnie who, just days ago, had reaffirmed to me the love she felt for Martha as we said our final farewell to her.

Juan got up to hug me and said, "Well, baby, I guess we are going to continue to do what we can. You are not alone. Remember, *No Estas Solo*."

We laughed and I had a sigh of relief that somehow—I wasn't sure how—but Familia Unida would continue in memory of beautiful Martha who forever touched our heart. Her spirit for life and her dedication to wanting to address social inequalities would continue for as long as we could, thanks to my family whose love carried me when I became doubtful.

With faith, family, and many more volunteers at Familia Unida, we continued to serve and open more doors of hope. I heard the little voice inside me remind me that, yes, it would not be easy, but it is something I must continue doing. My faith was being tested. Martha gone, more people needed help, we had no money, I knew that I had limited skills and needed a lot of help and much experience and so much more—my list was long for all the reasons to give up. However, my faith and my family were right—and maybe Miss Martha was sending me a message too. This is all I needed to make the decision to keeping moving forward. One day at a time. Yes, there was a long list of what I didn't know, but I also believed that with God in my heart, he would guide me and take me to all the places that I needed to go.

"Death and Life happens every day, we have right now to make a positive difference so do it now as later will soon be gone". Simply Amor

Chapter 14

Media Sparks More Awareness

*E*arly one morning in late September, I received a telephone call from one of the Familia Unida members who wanted to inform me that that there was a big article in one of the largest English language newspaper about MS and the correlation between bee stings. She urged me to read it and learn about this new treatment option. Soon thereafter, I saw a major newspaper article and learned about this alternative optional treatment for multiple sclerosis. I became excited that there were different types of methods for addressing a cure or treatment.

The article contained a photo of a Caucasian woman giving herself a bee sting on her arm. As I read the article in its entirety, I was reminded that there was no mention about cultural implications or references to the effects to people of color, or specifically, the Spanish-speaking community.

I began to think of the Spanish-speaking members that were at my home just a few days ago, who sat on my living-room couch in tears because they were very much confused about what was happening to their bodies. Their MS affected their ability to walk, caused slurred speech, and created depression. We hugged and cried and I tried my best to translate the English language brochures. The English language materials described there was no cure, and that studies stated it wasn't known if MS was environmental or hereditary. What was clear was that the brain and central nervous system were connected to all the vital organs that could be affected at any moment. The medical terms conveyed a brain with different nerve fibers and lesions on the brain; terms I was not sure how to translate accurately. Well, maybe I did say they were "lesions," but even I wasn't sure what all this really meant.

I felt an immediate urgency that told me that I needed to find Frank del Olmo who was an editor at one of the nation's largest English-language newspapers, the *Los Angeles Times.* "Who is Frank?" my husband asked...when I told him to inform him that I was going to drive to downtown Los Angeles and see if he can help bring awareness by having articles written about the Spanish-speaking Familia Unida members who are urging materials in Spanish to fully understand the terms I was saying or read in the English-language materials that their doctors gave them at the hospital.

Juan said, "Okay, well, be careful driving downtown."

Within minutes, I changed from my comfortable sweats into a colorful dress. I gathered my photo album that showcased some of our members who went to the monthly support group meetings. The gray and black photo album also captured some of my home gatherings, the volunteers and my family sorting food for the pantry. I went back into my house right before I was about to drive away to also take the poster board that had more photos of our beautiful Familia Unida members at gatherings that highlighted Latino families and also included some of the commendations from elected officials who recognized Familia Unida Living with MS as the first MS organization to reach out to the Spanish-speaking community.

So now I was driving downtown alone and in traffic. I lived approximately 30 minutes from downtown, and I was feeling anxious and unsure of where I was going exactly. All I knew was that this well-known newspaper had an office close to Broadway Street, and I was going to find Frank del Olmo. If anyone will listen, it will be him because reading his editorials I knew that he was a major voice for the Latino community and the first Latino executive editor and nationally known columnist and Pulitzer Prize–winning journalist for this reputable newspaper.

My heart was telling me that I must keep driving to the city of Los Angeles and to stop making excuses about the traffic. I told myself to stop procrastinating and stop thinking about being rejected because I didn't have an appointment and stop questioning myself as to how am I going to find him. No, I am *not* turning back, I told myself. I turned off the music because I did not want any more distractions. I had to pay attention to the streets, the one-way arrows, and the people who were walking in front of my car, even though they weren't supposed to.

I was driving on Broadway Street in Los Angeles. I smiled. Finally, I was at the *LA Times* newspaper building. My heart began to get excited as I saw its name in big letters written on the wall. However, I became confused as I noticed there were two newspaper buildings. Oh, great, how was I going to get inside?

I looked at both buildings that were right across from each other. How would I know which building to enter? I decided to make a turn onto the left building because it so happened that at that very moment there was a security guard busy talking with someone in a car at the entrance. This vehicle was in front of my car. I was going to wait until after their conversation ended to find out where I needed to go. However, my gut told me that if I asked the security guard where I could find Frank del

Olmo simply because I needed to speak with him, he would probably ask me if I had an appointment. Or worse—not tell me how to get inside that building because I knew that the electronic gate stopper was there for a reason. The gate lever was up, and I had a feeling that this was the entrance for employees or guests to go inside the building.

While the security guard continued to talk to the person who was in the vehicle in front of me, there was just enough space for me to go around the car and so I did what a person on a mission needed to do. Yup, this was my chance to sneak in!

I drove quickly and smoothly into the dark parking structure! My hands were sweaty, and I continued to travel up to another floor. I don't recall how many floors up I went. However, I began to pray and say, "Oh my God, please guide me to Frank del Olmo."

I looked at my rearview mirror, and thank you, dear God, the security guard from downstairs was not looking for me. I finally found a parking spot and felt a little bit better. But now, I needed to figure out how I was going to get inside the building. Where is the elevator? What floor do I ask for? Will I need a pass to get inside the building? Will they see me as a stalker? Well, in some ways, yes, it could appear this way. After all, Mr. del Olmo doesn't know me. I only know his name from his articles and columns. From what I got from his writings, he seemed to be a righteous, intelligent human being who had a passion for bringing awareness to the realities of Latinos, Mexicanos, and those who fell under the umbrella of speaking Spanish. He was an expert and shared a wealth of information about Latino history, present and future, and conveyed his knowledge in a manner that was comprehensive. He always made me laugh, smile, or feel proud to be Latina.

Okay, so now I am walking, and I am carrying my photo album, the poster board, and my purse. As I continued to walk like I knew where I was going and directly to my right side, I noticed a gentleman smoking by the entrance. He was a Caucasian middle-aged man standing against the wall taking a few puffs from his cigarette. As I got closer to him, he said "hello." I smiled and said hello back. Then I said, "I am looking for the level where Frank del Olmo is."

Then he said with a smile, you are on the right level, and immediately began to open the door for me. My heart skipped a beat. I smiled and said thank you so much as I walked into the floor where Frank del Olmo's office was. Can you believe this? Yes, I didn't have to get on an elevator or have to explain myself—well, not just yet.

The first thing I noticed were desks and some cubicles and women and men were rushing past me saying hello or smiling. Then one person asked me if I wanted a sandwich and I said no thank you. I continued to walk straight-ahead like I knew where I was going. I began to sweat some more and thought I must be blending in since they are asking me if I want a plate of the food. It appeared that there was a potluck or maybe it was lunchtime.

As I got closer to the end of the floor, I stood there for a moment, and a young Latina was watching me as she was carrying a plate of yummy food. She came closer to me and said, "Who are you?" I felt that she was the first person who saw me confused and out of place from the lunch atmosphere that was taking place all around me. She asked again. "Do you have an appointment with someone? Are you lost?" I said, "No, I do not have an appointment, and I kinda snuck in because I have wanted to speak with Frank del Olmo about Familia Unida." I began to show her my album and my poster. She listened and I could feel like she wanted to help. My entire body felt wet by then. I was perspiring, and it showed. *Yes, I am nervous and talking fast and didn't want her to kick me out* were my private racing thoughts.

The young confidante and pretty Latina thought for a few seconds more then smiled back at me and said, "It is your lucky day! Today is my birthday, and I am Frank del Olmo's assistant!" She continued to say, "I will ask him if he can see you briefly when he returns." She showed me where I could sit down and wait. She asked me if I wanted to eat something or if I wanted some water. I responded "No, thank you." My heart was beating fast, my stomach was in knots as I processed that I was actually going to see Frank del Olmo. How could I possibly eat anything when I needed to prepare? I still couldn't believe that I was sitting outside his office. I thanked her again for helping me and being so nice. She told me that he would be entering from that door (signaling to the right side) and that as soon as he came back she would let him know that I was waiting to speak with him.

As I sat waiting for him, I saw several people go in and out, and then I realized that I didn't even know what he looked like for sure, and possibly he had passed me already. The newspaper editorials had a photo of him, but today, I was drawing a blank, and I wanted to make sure that I was picturing the same person that I only knew by photo. I was nervous, and he would be coming in any moment. I went back to the nice woman and apologized and said, "I am so sorry, I know you said he would come from that door but I do not know what he looks like." She smiled and said, "I'll be right back."

I watched her as she went into a clear glass office and she took a photo from his office and brought it back to me and said, "Look, this is Frank del Olmo." I smiled in relief. He looked like the photos I had seen of him in the newspaper. I knew that I would recognize him once he walked in the door.

Moments afterward, he walked in the door and his assistant immediately approached him. She told him that I was waiting to see if I could speak with him. He looked at me a bit perplexed and with a faint smile, said, "You have 5 minutes" as he looked down at his wristwatch, and then proceeded to walk in front of me and led me into his clear glass office which I was admiring before he arrived.

He motioned for me to sit down while he came around to view the poster board that I positioned by the side of his desk. I shared about our Familia Unida members and why it was important for him to help bring awareness to the Spanish-speaking community living with MS who were disconnected from mainstream resources and support. I began to tell him about my diagnosis of MS, and how I couldn't walk and how I didn't ever want anyone to feel depressed or alone because they didn't understand this incurable disease that now exists in their body. I showed him the photos of the Familia Unida families and the urgent need to have materials available or accessible in Spanish and in a manner that was easy for the Spanish-speaking community to read. I went on and on talking quickly because I was sure I had gone over my 5 minutes.

Mr. del Olmo began to ask me more questions. I could tell that I had his attention by the way he leaned over, and then came around to sit closer to me as we viewed the photo album together. He nodded in agreement with my sentiment as I spoke about the outward institutionalized discrimination that kept many voices silent. He asked me more questions, and then pulled up his chair to echo similar sentiments and we exchanged experiences that were personal about our family. We also spoke about the need for more awareness surrounding Latino concerns, as well as the disparities in health and social services.

He smiled as he shared insights about his son who battled special medical needs. I looked at the clock and noticed that we had been meeting for almost 45 minutes. I said, "This was the best 5 minutes ever," and we both laughed! I apologized for taking up so much of his time that passed rather quickly. With all sincerity, I believed him when he said, he was glad that I came by.

He smiled and said, "You will be contacted by one of our reporters," and he gave me her name so that I would be sure to know that she was calling from the *LA Times*. He spoke with vindication, "Yes, Familia Unida will have an article in the *LA Times*" and smiled. His words were exactly what I wanted to hear. However, when he said it, I did not jump up and down like I pictured myself doing when I drove downtown that day. Instead, I felt an inner peace and a little exhausted. Maybe it was because Mr. del Olmo gave me the opportunity to share; he listened with heartfelt compassion and understanding. It was as though he understood that my community needed a voice and to be heard.

All I knew that morning before meeting him was that it was my ethical responsibility to relay the voices of the 40-plus Spanish-speaking members whose voices and testimonies longed to belong and be counted. He listened and appeared to comprehend the sentiments felt from a mom who had called me to share that her young son of Mexican descent was recently diagnosed with MS. However, she had shared in frustration that before getting to this conclusion of the diagnosis of MS the doctors and medical staff had first accused her of beating her son and hitting him on the head and that was why there were lesions on his MRI. The doctors and staff had treated her like she was a bad mother when, in fact, all along, his symptoms of MS were being ruled out simply because he was not Caucasian. Finally the medical team realized that, yes, in fact, the young boy had the diagnosis of MS.

When I shared with Mr. del Olmo about Martha who had lost her vision to MS complications and how she could no longer read the English language materials about MS or treatment options to her mom who only spoke Spanish, he shared many other similar sentiments and testimonies that he had experienced from families living with different types of illnesses and disabilities and who were Spanish speaking. When I spoke of the families who had contacted me from different parts of the United States and Mexico too, who desperately wanted someone to know that they too were living somewhere far away and also wanted to belong and be a part of this new movement called Familia Unida, he nodded and said, "Yes, their voices will soon be heard." We agreed that, yes, their voices of despair, confusion, sadness, and excitement were indeed valid. And, they were not alone.

I was thrilled to know that Frank del Olmo was going to help bring attention to those for whom I advocated. He said to me, "Thank you for what you are doing." He leaned over and picked up my items and walked me to my car.

The reporter that he said would call the next day did, in fact, call me the following day. I invited her to come to the next Familia Unida monthly support group meeting scheduled. The first *LA Times* article titled "Support Group for MS patients uses Spanish to reach out to Latinos" was published in the *LA Times* on October 11, 1998. Latinos and different ethnic groups affected by MS were now getting attention and materials in Spanish and were now an important topic for the medical community, and after the article appeared, positive changes were transpiring for the better.

"We never know how our actions will inspire others—surprises transpire and moments are treasured when acts of kindness are shared." Simply Amor

Chapter 15

Mentors Support—Helpful Tips I Learned

*C*ommunication is key to any relationship. Whenever you are feeling down, let those emotions come out in a safe way. For example, reach out to someone or pray and think of the healthy approaches that can result in a positive outcome. Be honest and ask yourself, why did I get upset, frustrated, or feel uncomfortable? Scream, cry, and understand the root of what is causing you distress. The sooner that you understand the triggers to your range of emotions, the quicker you will find ways to cope, improve, or change how to respond and address whatever it is that is affecting you in a negative or unhealthy manner.

I believe that the root of many illnesses and diseases comes from stressful experiences. How we either communicate or shut down will have a different outcome. For example, not having enough time in the day to serve my community, raise money, or change disparities in the many areas that were evident everywhere I turned caused me to become overwhelmed, which resulted in sleepless nights. My heart ached realizing that I didn't have the answers or resources to do it all. I had to learn to pick and choose, prioritize, delegate, and keep building more leaders. I needed to ask for help and deal with my own nourishment and health for proper balance and successful outcomes.

The Familia Unida team members collectively built more resources, did more advocacy, and I finally forgave myself for not being able to personally contribute everywhere I wanted to. I accepted that I was only one person doing what I could in one day and doing my best the next day and accepting that I was never going to please everyone all the time. I began to put my trust in God that many others were being touched to support all those that I could not possibly reach or assist. Familia Unida could not possibly reach all that kept calling throughout the country and beyond as a sole supporter. Eventually, I understood that I would never be able to please all the people all the time. However, as a board we are cognizant that with more financial assistance, expert leaders and more community partnerships, Familia Unida's will continue to flourish and serve with the spirit of happy and loving hearts. I continue to strengthen a successor plan that will translate to longevity and On a daily basis I am reminded that more financial resources and experts in all fields are needed so that we can continue with the blessings of service through Familia Unida's mission and the continuation of our motto: "You are not alone, no estas solo".

Yes, I have many areas to still develop and learn and I am open to grow and encourage everyone to never stop learning and growing. I found comfort in prayer and putting it up to God to handle when I knew I was not capable of doing so. I could not take away others' pain or illnesses, but I could be a good friend that loved them. I would share my expertise and mentor more young and old leaders who had the compassion and spirit to make a difference. This didn't mean that I was going to stop trying or serving. No, on the contrary, it gave me the ability to take away the negative or sad moments that I was holding on to because my heart ached that I could not help all that had crossed my path.

In time, I realized that it was okay for me to feel happy that my diagnosis or illness of living with MS was in remission or not progressing. When I began to feel happier and thankful for feeling not simply good but actually great because my diagnosis of MS had improved dramatically, I had much more energy to make even a small dent in my service to others and I learned to celebrate each bench marker, as small as it was. I began to comprehend that I may not have all the answers and that I felt compelled to learn to do better. I reached out more and more to others to fill in the gaps where I knew I couldn't. I gave myself permission to take a vacation that was long overdue and that I deserved.

Yes, I also needed to rest and have a break so that I could be of better service and enjoy myself. I began to let go of the guilt for feeling good health despite many of my Familia Unida friends who continued to get worse or progressed in a downward spiral. I continued to pray and ask for God's guidance and support to all who I knew were facing another a new crisis—or worse—had lost their loved one and were now alone.

It was true, that I could not resolve or fix it all, but now I felt strength in knowing that I will do what I could as best I could and encourage others to do the same. My sadness and stress came from not understanding the emotional triggers. Once I saw clearly that there was so much that I had no control over I was able to rest and rejuvenate and continue on this amazing journey. What I learned in this process was that if my stressors caused me to eat because I could not take away one of our member's pain, then I had to stop myself and say, "If I continue to overeat, then I will develop other illnesses such as diabetics, high cholesterol, or worse, give myself a heart attack—and what good would I be to myself and others if I am causing myself to be in a worse condition than to be healthier?" I weighed myself several years ago and calculated that I had put on many extra pounds, okay, I will be more exact. I gained approximately ten pounds every year that I lost a member living wit MS. Over the years I put on an additional 125 lbs. I carried a little bit of them with me and sadly each year I lost someone else. It has taken me years to learn that I deserved to be as healthy as I could. I am finally investing in me as much as I am investing in my community. I am finally eating better, having more balance, taking more breaks and still pushing myself to do more exercise but aware that this is my weakness. I am aware of where I can be better with caring for me as I have cared for all who surround me. I love who I have become and stopped feeling guilty for not being able to do more for my friends who have passed away. I carry their greatness with me and save my energy for serving and for me too!

For many years in my passion to serve, my stomach became upset because I could not give one of our members the money she needed to pay her phone bill, then I had to rationalize this emotional trigger to research appropriate resources to assist with this urgent concern for someone in need, rather than cause my body to act out and feel nauseated or cause myself to create a pain or cramp because my stomach muscles were tight. This tightness in my stomach could then lead to feeling constipation as my body told me exactly what kind of emotion I was feeling. Therefore, when I relaxed, drank my water, and listened to my music, massaged my doggies and gave my body healthy nourishment, that was when my dry skin began to glow and my hair was no longer dry and my body felt in balance.

Stress can cause our insides to feel yucky. Stress in my case resulted in me becoming overweight, not doing enough exercises, and having poor eating habits. I was skipping meals because I was extremely busy, or rushing and not paying attention to what I was giving my body for nourishment. Therefore, being in check with myself on a daily basis and with the support of Beth Zachary, president of White Memorial Medical Center and her team of wellness educators, it helped me to reinforce what I already knew I had to do...and kept putting off.

Becoming more health conscious has been an interesting journey and one of the most difficult assignments because I love to eat and enjoy delicious flavors and spices. I understand better what my triggers are that cause me to overeat. Therefore, I am making better choices...most of the time. It is not easy to be in check of how many times food is eaten as it can happen quickly and without thought.

Sometimes it was easy to pretend that I was not overeating. In other words, not pay attention to how many times I had a snack or noticing how late it was in the evening that I was preparing a *quesadilla,* a tortilla with cheese and salsa snack. However, my body did a good job in bringing me back to reality when my clothes did not fit comfortably... or didn't fit at all. So my first rule was that I needed to be totally honest with myself and come to terms that I was having an intake of many more calories and not burning enough calories. Being honest with what we are eating and drinking can help us to make better-informed choices.

Some may feel anxious or an anxiety from feeling overwhelmed with all that transpires in one day. I like to write out my list of what I plan to accomplish. Oftentimes, I only get to 25 percent of what is on my list of assignments because life happens and other tasks or new urgencies take me in another direction. What helps me is that I continue with my to-do list and whatever I didn't finish on that particular day is added to my new day the following day. I continue to do what I can from the list of the previous day. There is no use staying up late at night wondering what I will do tomorrow or feel horrible for all that I didn't do that I planned to do. I accept that I am not perfect, that I am doing the best that I can, and I give myself permission to start over again the next day and check off my to-do list.

I like to pray throughout the day and ask God for strength or clarity or patience or whatever it is I need at that moment. This helps me to tune in to what I am feeling and also gives me an opportunity to work through whatever is taking place and either ask for help, delegate it, or do what I can to improve the feeling of stress that I felt coming and especially, help me to focus on my list of priorities that may get rearranged throughout the day. However, as long as I can refer to it, it helps me to know that this is important.

The more I began to journal my assignments; it also helped me to also evaluate my feelings and experiences that transpired throughout the day. Taking time out to process each day helped to slow me down. The sooner that I understood what triggered negative feelings, such as sadness, despair, or frustration, the sooner I was able to address it and come to terms with what I could realistically do to improve the situation.

Keep in mind that the more you do this, the more you will discover that we pretty much don't have much control over anything or others. Therefore, find the goodness of what was good in all negative experiences. I believe that there is something good that can come out of whatever it is you are feeling. Communicate what you are feeling, especially with your loved ones whoever that may be. Don't try to go through anything alone. I like to pray and talk to God and ask for guidance when I have questioned my direction or when I sought affirmation. Almost instantly, I saw what I was supposed to see or hear what I was supposed to hear, simply by taking a moment to process and ask for help. I didn't always do this, but in my discovery of myself, I became more spiritual as I found myself in situations where I needed counsel or guidance, and God has been my first best friend.

Oftentimes when we really need guidance or find ourselves stressed, depressed, or overwhelmed—or all three—it is easy to shut down, pretend we are okay, and it's at that moment that I had realized that I was not sleeping well, eating way too much, and isolated myself from those that I knew would support me if only I let them in. So please, don't shut out family and friends or God if you are a spiritual being. Our lives and days can be so differently played out based on how we decide to be. So don't think you are the only one that goes through "stuff." Remember that we all go through "stuff" at some point in our day or weeks or months and even for years. I say to you, get yourself out of that frozen block of ice wall that makes you cold, insensitive, and numb to what is happening to you. Let your warm heart melt away the frozen ice wall, and guess what? Before you know it, you are gleaming and shining, and then you will attract other great energy. This is the point of excitement when you will see that possibilities are endless!

When you believe in you and you decide it's time to make a positive change, your inner you that has been wanting to come out...but waiting for you to give it permission to, finally comes out and will remember how good this feels. During this realization is when you can be free again to smile, laugh, and create more beautiful experiences. Love is contagious, so please, *let yourself be that..*

Naturally, there will always be something to be sad about. Well, I say, snap out of that by changing negative thoughts to positive ones. It's not that easy but easier than you think. Even if you are not sure if this will work (I am speaking to the skeptics), think honestly of the gifts that you have right in front of you. It may be as simple as telling yourself, "Well, I am thankful that I have my vision, my speech, I can walk, and I have a brain that allows me to realize that it's not so bad after all." And for some, this is not so simple because of circumstances that have affected their vision or speech or ability to travel due to limited resources, illness, disability, or other reasons that seem too impossible to do.

Keep in mind that not all have persons have the ability to walk, speak, see, or even get out of bed due to illness or disability. If you have choices to use your brain, can have friends, and may have experiences that can make you comfortable, then you also have the ability to experience beautiful moments. Our brain is powerful and magical and can take us to many wonderful places. *Choose life and lovely days.* We all have a purpose and can find peace, so please, find your purpose for peace and balance.

From my experience I have found that the more that I shared my passion with acquaintances or new friends, chances are they also have similar interests, values, or simply a kind heart to embrace a great idea. Some of those new persons evolved into wonderful friendships, partnerships, and individuals who also brought more great friends to support a goal. The vision becomes a reality not from the vision of one but the reality for many. Therefore, when you are requesting assistance, support, and when the communication is clear, more brains are building something wonderful!

One of my weaknesses early on was not feeling comfortable asking for support in the many forms that I needed. I found it especially difficult to ask for financial assistance to strengthen the capacity-building efforts, to serve better and to assist more families through Familia Unida. I was too proud and felt embarrassed or incompetent because I still had so much to learn. I finally gave myself permission to learn. I see now what I wished I saw many years ago. *It is okay* to delegate appropriately or conceptualize that learning is ongoing and that I do not have to do it all myself.

There are many capable persons ready to help. My case in point, I wish I would have learned this lesson early on because now, years later, I see that it's extremely important to ask for help and not carry the load with a few helping hands...when we can have hundreds—or even thousands more. The mentors who have surrounded me in this important process have shared of their heart and expertise on countless occasions, and, yes, I listened and took some great advice—finally! However, I did not fully see the value of these important relationships or knew how to best explore the possibilities that were right there in front of me.

In retrospect, I realized even more now how valuable this support was priceless, and, no, it's not too late to keep learning and growing and making mistakes. That's where friends in all aspects of knowledge are priceless and needed, as the more you know, the more you can delegate appropriately to great people and trust building becomes stronger. The key to success is clear communication, follow up, and beginning with short realistic goals and objectives that keep you on a focused path. So oftentimes your family or friends don't know that what they know you don't know and therefore, may assume that you know something that you don't know. Hmm, so when someone asks you, "How can I help?"... share the situation. It's okay to share, "I have never done that before" or share some examples of how this can work. If someone says, "I am not an expert in that area," Don't leave it at that. It's okay to ask, "Do you know someone else who is?" If so, the next question should be, "Can you connect me to that person, make a phone call, or send an e-mail on my behalf?"

Perhaps the person will say, "I am unable to support you at this time but can assist with an in-kind donation or possibly ask my colleague or someone else I know to assist." What I am saying is the more that your friends know that you need help, then and only then do you give them an opportunity to invite others to help that you may not even know about or realize the beauty of this gift until this transpires. This can build your circle of friends to include more expertise and support as you identify goals and objectives and more unintended positive outcomes transpire. Where there is good intention, goodness will follow.

Time is of essence so maximize your time and efforts so that you may have time for yourself to rest and recharge and, yes, mini vacations and long vacations will rejuvenate you and help keep your spirit, body, and soul refreshed and ready to do it again! It is important to mention too that this may also enhance your creative side that sparks great ideas, especially when you are having fun! An expression of gratitude or a simple "thank you" to someone that came through for you goes a long ways.

Oftentimes, we get so busy and caught up with a text or an e-mail or leaving a voice mail, or worse, we get so busy with the project or assignments that are "urgent" and forget a very key act that will possibly strengthen our community-building efforts. So please remember to take the time to say thank you because we often defend our excuses for not saying thank you by justifying our actions of forgetting or being too busy to say those two little, yet meaningful words. We say, "Well, he/she already knows I'm thankful and we don't have to say it because he or she already knows this and why we are friends." Yes, that may true and some will say that when we give from the heart we don't need a thank you, and I must be contradicting myself right now because I find myself doing a lot for others and a thank you was not expected and not the purpose of why I did what I did. However, I will tell you that the more time I take out to demonstrate gratitude and say thank you with a note mailed to her/him, the more I am also able to give more because taking time for the little things does lead to bigger and stronger and healthier relationships.

Gratitude means feeling grateful and the feeling is a great one. Therefore, taking time out to write a nice note and sending it in the regular mail is a nice and unexpected surprise. Small acts of kindness go a long way. Never stop saying thank you and showing gratitude to all who have inspired you, especially those that you don't know personally but have somehow impacted a spark of happiness or who have taught you some valuable lesson. Strangers love hearing about how they somehow touched you in some positive way.

I have selected 14 of some of the special friends that have inspired me as part of my acknowledgments page. Please take time to read about them. I said I selected 14 and I am reminded of many more special experts who became great friends in the process. Maria Nelson stands out as another Sheroe. Maria shared of her legal expertise and mentorship pro-bono for many years as needed., thanks also to Jones Day. Maria's guidance and support especially with trademarks and copyright counsel was priceless. I urge you to develop an acknowledgment journal that is filled with special thoughts of those that have touched you. Update it each year and share it with that person and others, highlighting special experiences and bench markers. It is healing, rewarding, and focuses our energy in positive messages. Try this at least once a year and share your thank-you message with them because taking time out to process and remember who touched you and why they touched you reinforces your love and gratitude. I'm sure your thank-you message will put a smile on their face. If the person you are thinking of has passed away or moved away and you think that the message will not reach them, I say you are wrong!! Write it anyway, share special memories with family and friends and acknowledge those that have passed. You honor them keeping their lovely spirit alive. Their legacy will continue.

We need more positive energy, so remember to choose healing words when speaking, and, yes, we will have bad days and sad moments, but healing words can change the mood and turn those sad and negative thoughts into fun or funny and lovely moments. Continue to find the positive in every situation and look closely because there is something positive that we can see when we want to see it. Choose to see and you will believe.

"Mentor someone and share your talents for a greater you and community." Simply Amor

Chapter 16

Mexican Sabor

A taste of Mexican *sabor* (flavor) is who I am. I do believe that our cultural influences and traditions are the core to our identity. Throughout the years I have noticed myself embracing my cultural identity more and more and proudly share my traditions, culture, and insight to who I like to be. When you come to my office you will notice colorful streamers hanging from the ceiling that appear like I just had a birthday celebration in my office. If you are visiting for the first time I will welcome you by saying *"Felicidades"* (Happy Birthday) and express to you, " live your day like it is your birthday! Full of happiness and with a feeling you get when there is a celebration that you enjoy!"

I share my philosophy when I describe my office colors. Like the lime green, fuchsia, and purple walls that are colorful and painted throughout the Familia Unida office space creates good energy. I'm not sure why, but for me, being around colors attracts a good feeling like no other. Keep in mind that our office is located inside a county facility that has beige walls and a conservative appearance—that is, until you find yourself at the Familia Unida office that engages you. The Familia Unida loving approach to service is contagious!

Sometimes our counselors will come into my office with a heavy heart or feeling overwhelmed from just meeting with a client who shared their crisis situation. Our Familia Unida team knows that they can come and sit in my office for as long as they need to, to remember our mission. Sometimes we are serving families who are now homeless, whose disease is progressing and becoming more incapacitating, or who have just experienced a divorce or the passing of a loved one. They have many stressors. We are reminded of our limited budget that currently doesn't allow us to serve the many more that are on the waiting list for home visits.

We have had to narrow our focus as to how many places we can physically go to serve until our core operational gaps are stronger. I reinforce to our beautiful team that we may not be able to take away our clients' illness or pain or go to all of them that are further away or who require a home visit because their illness has made it impossible now for them to come to us, maybe not today, but our prayers are that soon this will be a reality. However, right now, we can be a listening ear, share our heart, and treat them with respect.

I sometimes have to remind our beautiful Familia Unida teams that their personalized care to providing information about resources, especially through a loving message, is felt and lets others know that someone cares. So, when our teams think that they are not doing enough I like to remind them of how love opens hearts and is healing.

When our members come to our office it usually ends with a hug because the touch of love and kindness can also heal a broken heart. I always reinforce to our team and tell myself too that we cannot take home their pain and sadness. To be of service to others we need to be strong enough to feel their heart and sorrows but not too sad that it prevents us from being of service and support. We must serve as best we can, then go home and rest, knowing we have accomplished something important and that we did what we could.

I stress that we must forgive ourselves for not knowing it all and reaffirm the importance of reaching out to others that have expertise and a kind heart. The importance of remembering to communicate feelings is key because our emotions become our actions, and our thoughts become who we are. I remind our beautiful team that they must give themselves permission to go home and rest and smile and be present for their family or allow themselves to celebrate the greatness that is inside of them, even if their assistance seemed so small, or in their words, just a tiny act of kindness. We must remember these things instead of focusing of what we didn't accomplish, because we did the best we could have. Remember, you can always make it better with the desire to do so.

Allow yourself to be okay with hearing beautiful music after a long day of feeling that possibly you could have done better. Don't beat yourself up because you didn't finish it all. Hello! That's why we are given another day to start all over again and make this next day a day filled with quality and care. I trust that all happens as it should. So, as long as you gave it your best shot, allow your thoughts to create happier thoughts and memories. Give yourself permission to rest or be attentive to yourself and your family, friends, pets, and those who you hold close to you.

Recognize all the blessings that you gave through the linkage to various resources, guidance, and support if you work in the human service field. Those that we provide services for do not want our pity. They come to us because we remind them that they are important and not alone. We may not have all the right answers, but when you serve from a healing heart it is felt, and so, we do what we can for as long as we can.

Spanish music, for me, is the most romantic sound that gives me warm fuzzy feelings. I recall my memories of growing up and special moments with my family and Juan. Therefore, I listen to it often and create an environment that feels good.

The delicious spices and *salsita* (homemade chili sauce) that I still enjoy making from my *molcajete* (rock dish for mixing and mashing chilies and spices by hand instead of by a blender) that my mother gave me years ago is still used at home to prepare delicious homemade salsa that I enjoy making for my family and friends who come ready with their jar from the last gathering for a refill of *"Mama Irma's Salsa."* Our family and friends' gatherings include traditional food mixed with all kinds of fusion taste representing anything that tastes delicious. Good music on a regular basis is soothing. My concept of a family, "Mexican *sabor*" (Mexican flavor), includes many beautiful people representing a variety of cultures, religious beliefs, sexual orientations, and gender, as well as my Mexican identity and flavor (*sabor*). The many delightful friendships I have, special traditions, and food have become a part of my identity as well.

All of these "flavors" are naturally rooted in the founding and existence of Familia Unida Living with MS. During our monthly support group meetings we dance to music usually led by Andy Padilla, a longtime board member, my soul brother and lifetime friend, volunteer, and healthcare provider who bridges exercise to Zumba or Salsa (a type of dancing) and funny jokes. Andy is a reminder that laughter is healing. We often share in a delicious potluck that features Mexican, American, Asian, and Soul food mixed with whatever our dinner sponsor adds to the delicious meal.

Mexican *sabor* also includes my special friend Mandy Wu, who I refer to as my younger sister. She is a counselor and patient advocate who loves sharing important resources and information with her clients. She provides insight to Chinese traditions while sharing a vegetarian hot or cold meal for our members. Mandy's love is transparent and includes her mom's help and that of the temple where she worships and prays for her "Familia Unida."

We sing out loud to the chicken dance that Andy leads while I serenade our Familia Unida members who are celebrating a birthday. Each month there is also someone who is treated to the singing of the *mananitas* (Happy Birthday in Spanish). We laugh when some feel like crying...Like when one of our members with progressive MS says with a big smile on her face, "I always have a seat wherever I go" referring to her wheelchair that keeps her mobile while she travels to many places.

Karina and Lena, Polly and others, smile and dance from their wheelchair seats and Norma also dances from simply moving her eyes and letting out a faint smile due to her limited physical mobility that prevents her from using her arms, shoulders, legs, or voice. Her body is very still, but her smile, though faint, is vibrant, and her eyes tell us she is having a lot of fun. We learn from each other in a safe and nonjudgmental manner that encourages more dialogues about our insecurities and our biases, and we are reminded that we are not so different after all.

A tradition that I began over 11 years ago was the Familia Unida Wheelchair Wash Day. We roll out the red carpet for the VIP guest that represents individuals living with different disabilities and showcase their many abilities. The red carpet is there for them to make a grand entrance and be welcomed by various spiritual leaders, as well as corporate and community friends that join on each side of the long red carpet entrance to cheer them on, and some offer a blessing and an act of kindness. The members that roll in to the Wheelchair Wash feel the excitement and share a smile while they are treated to a serenade given by mariachis and greeted by the spiritual leaders from various religious beliefs and cultural backgrounds who come together. This special day is at no cost and is open to the general public. All are welcomed to participate in the activities. The Familia Unida Wheelchair Wash and Health Awareness Day begins from early morning to late in the afternoon and is hosted in East Los Angeles.

The concept of the Wheelchair Wash was born when I first began to use a wheelchair. I had noticed that some wheelchairs were not as clean as mine. My girls and husband would help me to scrub and detail my wheelchair, and we had a lot of fun cleaning it together. I began to notice other people's wheelchairs once I owned one; I began to notice their scooters as they passed me while out in the community. I noticed some were attractive; others were newer models, while some were smaller or not as nice and needed fixing. One thing that I began to see more and more as I began to pay attention to other wheelchairs and electric scooters was that oftentimes, more than just a few were very dirty. I began to wonder why that was. Then I remembered that some of my mobile friends lived alone, others had limited mobility, some were visually impaired, and most simply could barely transfer to the wheelchair, so trying to clean up the wheelchair could result in an accident or become a hazard to their health given their strength limitations, illness, or disability.

I thought of the germs and the importance of health and wellness and germs turning to bacteria that lead to illness and so on. Therefore, in an effort to help my mobile friends, I shared that one day very soon Familia Unida would have a wheelchair wash cleaning day. I envisioned volunteers gathered to give the wheelchairs a detailed cleaning and tune-up. This day finally became a reality, and 22 friends came to our office to have their wheelchairs washed. More community members became interested, like hairstylists and beauty professionals who were inspired to offer a manicure or makeover. Then, like a chain reaction, more relationships and friendships were made and more compassionate volunteers came together to offer health resources, including a massage.

Today, the wheelchair washday also includes a health awareness and community fair, live music, delicious food, resources, and so many more surprises. Over 2,000 community members and their families and friends attend this commemorative celebration! Every year, the wheelchair washday attracts many more people than the previous one, thanks to corporations, communities, and elected officials. Healthcare providers and friends from all over the place come together to make a positive difference for the many more attendees that will remember this day for a long time. There is no cost for the participants to enjoy a special day that is dedicated to them during the month of July as we celebrate the Americans Disability Act and Disability Awareness Month. This special day reaffirms that we are not so different after showcasing that all people have many abilities.

"Open your mind and heart to feel what someone else feels that you perceive as different from you and find the similarities." Simply Amor

Chapter 17

Mi Sueno (My Dream)

Mi sueno, my many prayers and dreams since living with MS, had been that a cure be found for multiple sclerosis. When I was initially diagnosed with MS in the mid-1990s, treatment options were at the beginning phase of becoming available. I am reminded that back then there was no Internet, Facebook and the many other technology devices and social media outlets that bridge people, resources and countless of opportunities. In the early 1990's I depended on the public phone or the library in my community for learning. Many more inventions and methods to belong and feel connected.

Today, so much hope and many more alternative treatment medicine is available all over the world! It has been exciting for me to witness the many advancements and choices for MS patients, and especially alternative treatment options that bring comfort to patients diagnosed with MS. It's exciting to learn about the positive implications from meditation, yoga, and chiropractic therapy that some have said helped them to tolerate and reduce pain. Materials about MS and other illnesses are now made available in multiple languages and the Internet has been an invaluable source of information and enables people to be connected.

I continue to share insights of the power of love, faith, and spirituality that can also bring comfort, especially to those special folks that think they are alone, and who are suffering in isolation, without technology advancements due to fear, lack of resources or limited mobility. Some of our members live alone and return home to an empty dwelling. My biggest desire is to tell the world about the power of love and God that is in your heart.

I began to write a draft for a book over 14 years ago. However, due to my many excuses, you know...not enough time, maybe next week, maybe next year. The list of excuses is endless...I don't have the money, or worse, who will want to read my book when there are many good books available and I don't even have the time to read the books that I wish to read. Besides, my grammar is just "okay" and not good enough like the real authors I have read about.

Over 14 years ago I started penning my thoughts, my deep feelings— and deleted them. I started again with journal entries to capture the important experiences. As much as I wanted to finish it, I never seemed to find the time. It was also difficult to revisit some of my past that took me to reflect on some of my MS friends who had passed away throughout this process and yes, I still carry them in my hearts and yes, I miss them in the physical world. I find comfort in knowing that they are no longer suffering and believe that one day, when it's my time to go too, we will reunite and rejoice.

Today, I think I understand why I couldn't finish writing my book, and you will learn more about this in the final chapter.

Now I can finally finish my book that I started so many years ago. I have shared some of the experiences that shed insight to my background, history, challenges, and blessings that keep the Familia Unida office open and me alive today.

As I have shared previously, I started Familia Unida because of my diagnosis of multiple sclerosis and experiencing firsthand the need for support to the Spanish-speaking community. Each chapter was titled with words that had an M and an S. However, the M and the S represented other words that were not multiple sclerosis. I continued to reinforce throughout this book that MS did not have to represent multiple sclerosis; MS can represent many words, so I, instead, choose healing words to communicate and create positive conversations and helpful experiences. I think that there is some truth to "the words that we use to identify ourselves are who we become."

A beautiful leader and dear friend shared with me recently that she was a survivor of cancer. I applauded her for her strength and the many blessings that she is to many, including me. I told her that when I described her and thought of her I didn't think of the word *cancer*. Instead, I described her in the many other C words that illustrate, to me, who she is. Lillian is courageous, compassionate, charming, charismatic, cute, and many other C words that represent my beautiful friend. I made her laugh. She too was reminded of all the ways that she is a champion, and she agreed that she liked the C words and the new associations to the letter C.

So I ask you to remember the beautiful parts of what makes you. Do not focus on the faults that we sometimes find and magnify, that others don't see. Do not think of the worries; don't dwell on our heartaches or the pain that comes to us or through our body. Instead, find other feelings that are positive to embrace that will bring a smile, laughter, and peace of mind.

The literature and MS news is hopeful regarding MS advancements for a cure, and so we must find hope and healing wherever we can. Keep the faith and surround yourself with many loving hearts and communicate your feelings so that you understand your emotional triggers and change attitudes because we can choose to feel sad or mad or be happy and at peace despite all the reasons to feel down. Instead, find double, or even triple, the number of reasons to be happy!

For years, I have dreamed and have envisioned my body free of multiple sclerosis. When doctors or patients had dialogues with me about MS, some said, "Oh, you too have MS," or "How long have you had MS?" or "You have MS like me." I clarified to them that I did not claim the illness; I did not say that I "had MS"; I said instead, that I was "diagnosed with MS." It was important for me that I never said, "I have MS." I didn't want to claim it by saying that I had it. Instead, I merely said I have the *diagnosis* of MS. Why was that so important to me? Maybe it was because I did not want to accept this illness. I didn't want to own it or claim it or be the focus of conversations or simply let "MS" be the word that defined my identity. Maybe it was easier for me to live with it by not owning it.

I have lived with this diagnosis of MS for over 21 years, and I have shared the message of hope to hundreds and thousands throughout those 21-plus years. I decided to identify with something much bigger than illness or disease. So, for example, all these years of living with MS, I researched new treatment drugs, I tried alternative treatment drugs, I found ways to lower my stress level through prayer and by staying out of the sun, by creating my space that embraces love, acupuncture by the one and only Dr. Wong, surrounding myself with positive energy, and loving people and giving out the best energy I could. I learned that love is contagious. I believed that there were other parts of my identity that did not associate with MS. My conversations did not have to focus on illness, pain, or progression of the disease.

In order for me to continue to be a servant to my community, I focused on the strength of those served, their accomplishments, and their love and zest for life. I continued to be a supporter from the strengths' perspective. In other words, looking at the goodness that transpires from all our experiences regardless if they were sad or happy ones.

So many years have passed from when I was diagnosed with MS. The summer of 1990 to now has flown by swiftly. I went from not being able to walk when I was in my late 20s and from having limited strength in my hands and legs that resulted in my use of a wheelchair, and bladder dysfunction, dizziness, spasms, and pain that would travel throughout my body that sometimes started at my head and traveled all the way down to my toes. Major depression almost took my life. I felt helpless and that I was worthless or not good enough for my family. That was a time that I hope to forget. I mention it now and hope that this selfish act I did will help someone else to never give up, even in their darkest moments or when hope and isolation leads to wanting to disappear from the face of the earth. Remember that when we fall and fall hard we can *still* get up and start all over again. Please give yourself permission to belong and live, because there is a reason for why you are still here.

During the lowest point of my life was when I wanted to take my life. In a weird way this was also when I realized that we all needed to belong to something or someone. I learned that we have a purpose of why we are still here and if we do not communicate this feeling with someone, anybody, then, yes, we can succeed...with suicide, or worse, we will live but with a dead spirit and empty soul because we have not been able to find the way. The way to peace is rooted in love.

The first step to finding my path back to living my life with a purpose was me loving me despite my faults, forgiving myself for wanting to leave this earth, and regaining my faith and trust in God. If you believe in the power of prayer as I do now, then pray, ask for divine guidance and for the appropriate teachings so that you can learn how to be a better you. Go online (the Internet) and find resources, call Familia Unida, or tell a family member or even a stranger that you need help. You will never know what possibilities are out there if we simply give up and go into our invisible cave that you think is safe. Our mind is powerful for good and for evil too. Please choose life, and goodness and greatness will be yours.

It was during my darkest moments where I also felt the strongest. Maybe it came about from desperation to wanting to understand this new me, and it began with me forgiving me for wanting to give up on living.

"There is a reason for why we are here; find your passion and you will see many reasons for living." Simply Amor

Chapter 18

Multiple Sclerosis: Brief Facts

$\mathcal{I}$n the 1990s, treatment and medication were being developed to improve or stabilize the deterioration caused by multiple sclerosis. Therefore, my initial treatment only included dosages of steroids, physical therapy, muscle relaxers for the muscle spasms, or medication for the pain that I sometimes felt throughout my back that also traveled up to my head or sometimes I felt in my lower extremities.

The prognosis for the diagnosis of MS that I was told and read about is that *there was no cure*. No one knows how one gets it. Even today we don't know if it is environmental or hereditary. In the early 1990s, it was considered a mysterious illness. Back then, no research or information was available in Spanish and no data available as to the implications related to ethnic minority groups or the Latino community. My treatment for MS in the mid-1990s included prednisone (steroids), physical, and occupational therapy. I was excited to learn that in the near future treatment medication would be available in the United States.

My research in the demographics, and especially in the Latino community, in the early 1990s and throughout my research in the years to follow found that there were some individuals and ethnic communities that lacked awareness or support of resources, treatment, and overall support. My findings demonstrated that prior to the founding of Familia Unida Living with MS, national MS organizations had limited resources or research related to Latinos living with MS. Familia Unida Living with MS brought awareness to this disparity and dedicated its mission to bringing awareness to the need for appropriate services and support to diverse ethnic groups. The founding of Familia Unida Living with MS brought national and international awareness to gaps in research and support to the Spanish-speaking community and the need for appropriate language and the urgent need to embrace services for all. My publication titled "Cultural Implications and Latinos Living with MS, 2001, Irma Resendez," gave insight to the Latino culture and experiences living with MS. This publication also challenged the United States Census that capture how many people are living with MS since there are many who are not counted due to language, cultural, and institutional barriers, and many who are undocumented who are not counted at all, yet they still exist today.

Symptoms of MS

In multiple sclerosis, damage to the myelin in the central nervous system (CNS) and to the nerve fibers themselves interferes with the transmission of nerve signals between the brain and spinal cord and other parts of the body. This disruption of nerve signals produces the primary symptoms of MS, which vary depending on where the damage has occurred.

<u>Most Common Symptoms</u> (although they vary):

Fatigue
Numbness
Walking (Gait), Balance, & Coordination Problems
Bladder Dysfunction
Bowel Dysfunction
Vision Problems
Dizziness and Vertigo
Sexual Dysfunction
Pain
Cognitive Dysfunction
Emotional Changes
Major Depression
Spasticity
Paralysis

<u>Less Common Symptoms</u> (which occur infrequently):

Speech Disorders
Swallowing Problems
Headache
Hearing Loss
Seizures
Tremors
Respiration/Breathing Problems
Itching

Diagnosing MS

At this time, there are no symptoms, physical findings, or laboratory tests that can determine if a person has MS. The doctor uses several strategies to determine if a person meets the long-established criteria for a diagnosis of MS and to rule out other possible causes of whatever symptoms the person is experiencing. These strategies include a careful medical history, a neurologic exam, and various tests, including magnetic resonance imaging (MRI), evoked potentials (EP), and spinal fluid analysis.

The Criteria for a Diagnosis of MS

In order to make a diagnosis of MS, the physician must:

- Find evidence of damage in at least two separate areas of the central nervous system (CNS), which includes the brain, spinal cord, and optic nerves, AND find evidence that the damage occurred at least 1 month apart, AND rule out all other possible diagnoses.

I agree, this is a lot of information to grasp. You may wonder why I am taking time to share all of this. I will finally tell you why, because now, today, I have news to share that challenge medical advancements, faith, and miracles.

"Your life is precious; don't get caught up with the worry and fear of the unknown or bad or sad news. Make loving experiences happen every day." Simply Amor

Chapter 19

Miracles Soar

As you may recall, it was in May of 1990 when my Mother's Day celebration did not feel like a celebration. This day felt like chaos and uncertainty that forever changed me. Now, 21-plus years later, I have shared some brief highlights of this journey living with multiple sclerosis.

Throughout this journey, I have seen different medical doctors and tried different treatment options. Some neurologists recommend the latest MS drugs that included daily, every other day, or weekly injections, medicine for the spasms, or vitamin D supplements or prednisone for when I experienced an exacerbation, which means while I was experiencing a decline or episode that caused me to be more fatigued than usual or when I noticed that I would fall down, and my foot would drop, or I would loss my balance. So, yes, I tried one of the treatment medications but stopped after almost 6 months of ongoing fever, liver damage, and horrible shakes throughout my entire body that affected my ability to get out of bed. Funny, how certain memories seem so vivid today.

My daughter Johnnie was a young child attending elementary school and was the most qualified at home to give me injections in my arm, stomach, butt, and other places that didn't have bruises.

I reflect back to when Juan tried to give me one of my first injections. He prepared the solution and shook it with one hand while I watched his rough hands delicately unwrap the needle and shake the solution. I sat on the daybed in my underwear and with my stomach displayed, ready for him to inject me with the fluid that he had shaken that contained medication in the tiny glass bottle. We were both silent right before Juan came—rather quickly—at my stomach so fast and hard—and, yes, he scared me as I jumped back quickly because he almost jabbed my right boob as I jumped away while he held on tightly to the syringe that had the fluid with the treatment medication! Yes, my breast! Juan came at me with that syringe and headed toward my breast! No, my breasts were not hanging down to my stomach. Seriously, I didn't think my breasts were endangered until then. I thought they were safe in my bra until Juan came quickly at me.

I yelled out to him, "Honey, what is wrong with you!! You almost injected me on my boob!" He did inject my stomach but in a fierce and nervous manner that hurt.

He replied in his soft, strong voice, "I'm sorry, honey. I can't do this."

That was the first—and last—time that he injected me. For the most part, I gave myself the injections and would feel horrible soon afterward. Then my entire body would shake out of control. My girls and I would pretend that "Mama's ride was about to start again" as they jumped on top of me and lay on me laughing with me as my body shook them while they were on top of me. Soon after those injections, beside the horrible side effect of shaking nonstop in all parts of my body, I would get feverish and felt weak for the entire day.

I don't remember how it started but my *mija* Johnnie would sit with curiosity and watch me give myself my injections, and she would remind me when it was the evening to give me another one. With her tiny delicate hands she shook the solution that she mixed with a shake and would observe my body marks and would find spots that were not bruised and would slowly and with patience inject me at the perfect place and it didn't hurt. She didn't appear scared. It was something she did as a matter of fact. Jacqueline, like her daddy, had no interest in being around Mama when this time came.

There came a point when I told my neurologist that it didn't make sense to me that something that was supposed to help by slowing down the progression made me feel even more horrible. On top of that, to learn that during my weekly or monthly blood evaluations, results showed that my liver was abnormal from this medication, which really concerned me. Especially since I didn't drink or smoke and my liver test results kept coming out abnormal. Finally, I made the decision to stop taking the medication and continued to monitor my blood work. Yep, guess what happened as soon as that medicine was out of my body? My liver results became normal once more.

When the neurologist recommended another medication to replace the one that gave me horrible side effects, my response was "No, thank you." How can something that was supposed to help me get better cause harm to my organs and keep me bedridden? I couldn't stay in bed. I had my girls that needed me awake and alert. If I was going to continue to be dedicated to helping others, I couldn't take this medication that forced me to stay in bed. Therefore, I made the decision to discontinue the treatment options and monitored myself. I knew that the heat caused me to feel dizzy or extra tired so I avoided being out in the sun. If I felt my legs and foot weak, then I rested or used the electric scooter to get around.

In these chapters, I have shared a few of the many experiences to show what happened. I have given you some insight into my life living with MS for over 21 years. Remember that I shared that over 14 years ago I wanted to finish my book but couldn't do that? It just didn't feel like the right time. I couldn't get to the final chapter and so some of my notes stayed saved on notepads and on my computer. What I am about to share next is something that I have been processing for more than 2 years. Now, I am ready to share this information.

I went to visit my neurologist for my regular checkup. She requested an MRI to monitor my progress and reviewed my past records from various hospitals and medical doctors that have seen me throughout the years. Approximately 4 months later, my same neurologist requested to do another MRI. I followed her instructions and another MRI was taken of my brain and spinal cord. I became worried about having two MRIs in such a short time. I worried even more when I received a notice to return for my follow-up neurologist appointment as soon as possible. I decided I did not want to return. Why? Because I was afraid of what the outcome would be. I told myself that I am in God's hands and that I would return to see her when I wasn't so busy. I continued to be busier than ever, and so I put off returning to the hospital for a review of my two MRIs.

My mother would remind me that it was important to find out why my neurologist kept wanting to see me and that my health was urgent, as urgent as I felt it was for me to assist many that I served and mentored. She said I too needed to take care of myself. After much contemplation, I promised my mom that I would return before the year was over. It was a few days before Thanksgiving when I finally returned to visit my neurologist and receive the results from the latest MRI.

My neurologist appeared excited to see me and was eager to speak with me. I was finally at peace with whatever she would have to say to me. I prayed in my car before I went into the building and asked God for courage to deal with whatever it was she needed to share with me. I reminded myself that no matter what happens from her news of my MRIs, my faith would carry me through.

My neurologist began to share that she had been studying my MRIs and also my past records. We discussed what I had experienced throughout the years and how in the past years I had returned again to be admitted to the hospital after another exacerbation that include pneumonia which weakened my body. I referenced that I had to take steroids again to address the inflammation and hopefully address the MS attack. We touched on how MS caused lesions on my brain and the inflammation was evident in my previous x-rays according to past reports. The CT scans and many MRIs before hers had confirmed my diagnosis of over 21 years. I looked right back at her and said, "Okay, tell me what is happening now."

She sat quietly for a brief moment and looked at me. Then she said, "Irma, I have good news to share! Come here and look at this MRI report." She pointed it out on the computer monitor. I looked at it, and she began to tell me that in both of the MRI films (photos of my brain) that she had requested, there was now *no evidence* of multiple sclerosis! I responded, "What do you mean?" She replied, "Well, yes, your past MRI reports state the contrary. However, I'm telling you that today, the two MRIs that I had done do not show any evidence of MS. *There is NO MS evidence in the MRIs, and your brain has no inflammation and looks great!*"

In shock and very much confused, I said, "So what about the scars, inflammation, and lesions that were there?" She thought of how to answer again and said, "Well, I am not sure what you had before, but whatever it was, it is now gone." I asked, "So what do I have or had?" She said, "It could have been a type of chronic encephalomyelitis (ADEM). However, if that was what you had, there is no evidence that it is there now."

I sat in disbelief, too shocked to comprehend what I was hearing. I asked again, "Please tell me what I have." She said with a smile and with conviction, "Absolutely nothing." She then asked me, "Irma, would you like me to keep the MS diagnosis on your records or take it out?" I shouted out, "Take it out!"

She talked about my next appointment that would not be for a while, and while she was talking I interrupted her to say, "I founded Familia Unida because of my diagnosis and all that I experienced and for many who are also living with MS and especially for the Spanish-speaking community and many who wanted to belong...My whole life and commitment was to MS all these years, and now you tell me I do not have this? How could this be?" She took a moment to answer and said, "Well, it could have been possibly a misdiagnosis." She went back to explain again what she shared earlier that it could have been another condition that mimics MS. I was so happy inside, I am sure, but that was not my reaction at that moment.

I left her office feeling numb. I even forgot to stop at the front desk to pick up my next appointment. I grabbed the prescription form where I had asked her to please write down what the possible diagnosis was, because I had already forgotten the name. On the prescription paper she handwrote, "Encephalomyelitis (ADEM)." She reminded me that even that diagnosis was only a possibility and she could not confirm it because the x-rays, MRIs, showed nothing.

Quickly, I rushed out of the medical facility and tried to get into my car. The door would not open. I clicked the door locks again with my key and still the door would not open. Then as I tried again to pull the door open I noticed a child's car seat in the backseat, and then I saw that the car was not black but a dark blue. I laughed to myself and realized that I was trying to get into someone else's car. I finally found my black car and sat for a few moments inside, replaying over and over again what the doctor had told me. I cried with disbelief and could not believe this news.

I immediately called my mother and told her that I finally went to see my neurologist after so many months of missing my appointments. She asked, "So what happened, what did she say?" I replied, "Mom, she said that my MRI says I do *not* have the diagnosis of MS and there are no more lesions or inflammation or scars and that I am fine." We both were silent. Then we both began to try to talk but our crying took over our words that we were trying to say. At the same time we began to laugh together. My mom said that God heard her prayers and now she could rest and go in peace. She has been living with various chronic medical conditions. She continued, "God has healed you because of your love for everyone else. I am so happy my daughter...God bless you, my daughter," and as she spoke I was still crying in shock.

The person that I called next was my husband. I didn't know if I should at first because I knew he was probably doing some construction somewhere on top of a roof or perhaps inside an attic. I told myself, no, I better wait until he comes home. However, I changed my mind immediately after I said that. I couldn't wait until he came home. That would be too long, and I didn't think I could wait that long.

Juan answered his phone immediately. I told him, "Honey, you will never believe what my neurologist just told me." I could tell that he was trying to get himself ready to hear bad news. He said in a serious manner, "What did she say?" His tone sounded sad. When I finally told him, his response was entirely different from my mom's. He said, "This isn't true. She made a mistake. How can this MS be gone? All the years, and all that we have gone through . . ." He began to speak louder and was upset, bringing up past memories, like these things had just happened yesterday. He said, "I think they need to take another x-ray." I said, "Honey, they already did two MRIs this year, and they both came out the same. No MS." He said, "Well, we need to have another one done." I tried again to help him to understand what she said, and he sensed that his reaction was making me disturbed. He changed his tone of voice and said, instead, "This was good news, baby." But he continued by saying that he still had a difficult time believing this and to this day, he is still processing this news and says it is hard to believe this because we know what we went through.

Juan finally told me that his biggest fear was, "What if it comes back, and then we need to prepare ourselves again?" My response was "Embrace this good news and don't live in fear of something that hasn't happened and will not." If it does, well, we deal with whatever happens just like we are doing now. Throughout the past few years, Juan finally shared recently that he is grateful that my health has been better and he doesn't worry for me as much like before. He said again, "If it comes back?" I expressed that I did not share his sentiments and if he wanted to hold on to the MS, well, that would be his choice. However, I had let the MS go out of my mind and body years ago.

When I called my sister Jackie after I spoke to my husband on that special day of hearing this news, Jackie cried and yelled out, "Sister, remember all those years and times that the doctors wanted to keep you on that horrible medication that made you sick and I kept telling you to stop taking it? Aren't you glad you listened to me?" She continued, "My heart always told me that you were healed a long time ago. Thank God you stopped taking it. That medicine could have made it worse." We felt a sense of peace. That evening, I called a family meeting with our daughters and shared the great news. Juan came home with a bouquet of red roses. We hugged, and I cried, and he seemed very much in shock. I knew that deep down inside he wanted to believe this great news but found it difficult to accept this, at least not on this day.

We celebrated Thanksgiving several days earlier than the traditional Thanksgiving Day and gave thanks to God for this news. To think that all these years our daughters quietly feared that they too may possibly be diagnosed with MS since oftentimes women and generations with girls have been prevalent to get this diagnosis is what some doctors told me or stated in MS articles. Then I recalled the scary long ago thoughts of when I wanted to end my life the afternoon coming home from my doctor's appointment when I thought my family deserved better...

So much has happened since that day that we received this wonderful news. During this time the economy was still very much in a crisis, some of our program's grants had ended, more families were coming to our office in crisis, Familia Unida outgrew its capacity to better serve, and then during all this turmoil, I was also contacted to consider taking a position as an executive director at another organization that would pay me a lucrative salary. I felt so many emotions transpiring at once.

I sat with my family during this early Thanksgiving dinner and had long and serious dialogues about what I, or we, should do next. My husband asked me, "Well, what do you want to do?" I replied, "I know that our personal finances have been tough" (we are not wealthy by any means, and Juan has been covering most of the monthly bills). I also knew that it was very difficult for me to continue to serve in the capacity of a volunteer, and, yes, I have credentials and qualifications to get other employment opportunities as they have come my way. However, my heart told me that God has healed me so that I can continue on this journey and be healthier and serve even better.

Therefore, all agreed, and our girls said, "Mama, we need to help you as who else will work without a salary all the hours you do?" Thank goodness we said that we have various nonpaid interns who receive college credit for their time with us representing various universities and majors from social work, psychology, sociology, business administration technology, communication, and so much more.

We have found creative ways to serve, and we were all in agreement that we are barely getting started to build up Familia Unida. As a family, we felt even more committed to serve than ever before. By the grace of God, I am here to continue to find more ways to touch more lives. We have outgrown our capacity, and I am so proud of the team that works alongside me, especially the countless hours of volunteers that surround Familia Unida.

Now that the MS is gone from my body, and through the grace of God, I will continue to serve him for as long as I can. I listen to the messages and the new vision that I see so clearly today that has given me an abundance of energy and health. It is telling me to keep sharing the love and support and bring awareness to the urgent needs to sustain and build healthier communities.

I can now give more of myself because my health is better. I can walk, run, and have strong legs and good balance, and my cognitive skills feel sharp. I no longer wear a diaper or need to use a catheter, and I can drive a vehicle without special pedals. I no longer wear leg braces or use a wheelchair. My two MRIs witness that, after over 21 years of living with MS, today, I do not have this diagnosis of MS. Past MRIs confirmed this diagnosis years prior. I have accepted this, and I am still working on finding out my new identity. I am the same person...or am I? I still serve my community, but it's different because now when I meet someone for the first time and they tell me, "I have the diagnosis of MS just like you" or "We share a special connection because of our diagnosis of MS," or "You understand me because you also have gone through what I have gone through." Yes, I *did* have the diagnosis like you...so I thought. Yes, I do understand what you have gone through... My heart and my passion are stronger than before because I want others to believe in miracles and remind them that the doctors may not have all the answers, and to please listen to your body that will tell you when a medication is not good for you and when it's time to get another referral.

My friend, *you* have choices too. Everything that I have become since my diagnosis changed my life. I now feel different and, yet, the same. I feel that my body has been healed. I want others to experience what I have. I want to support and especially share love to many who still don't know about Familia Unida. I want to help bring awareness to the medical and healthcare professionals and share that as a community we must pay more attention to our neighbors and strangers on the streets who you feel in your heart would benefit from a kind word or assistance. You may just be a great resource for what they need. I want everyone to understand that life is precious. I want us to slow down and offer more acts of kindness everywhere we travel. I want us to stop saying that, "No, I can't" or "I won't," and that "maybe someone else will help that person or that family." No! Stop saying that we are too busy or convince yourself that someone else will do it.

I asked the doctors and those individuals who are in the health care, social services fields, and in positions where they are serving their community to look into the eyes of their patients, clients, customers if only for a few seconds, and ask yourself, if this person, this stranger that is right in front of me was my mother, father, sister, brother, daughter, son, best friend, etc., how would I want them to be treated? How would you take care of someone that you loved with all your heart? This is how we should see those that are counting on us for assistance, whatever that might be.

To the individuals and families who are living with an illness or disability, I ask you to please ask more questions and learn more about what is happening to your body or your family. Continue to communicate and keep finding more ways to feel healthier and happier regardless of the pain and suffering. When we share we become stronger.

I continue to echo the sentiment to our Familia Unida members and our community at large that doctors do not have all the answers all the time and that we need to seek out second opinions and listen to our body and pay attention to changes often. We need to take responsibility for our bodies and feel and understand our bodies better.

My husband and I recently celebrated 30 years of marriage. He is still in shock that this good news could really happen. He was afraid to believe this. So, I went to see another neurologist and showed him my reports and MRI results and the second neurologist's response was, "Do not try to fix something that is not broken." I agreed and he said, "This is good news, and I am very happy for you and your family." I then went to see Dr. Saperia, who admitted me many years ago back in 1990. Throughout the years he served as a Familia Unida board member, advisor, and in the process, became my personal friend. I printed the old records and the news ones and he sat quietly and read and read while we had dinner at a nearby café by the rehabilitation hospital where I spent over 3 months. He ate, smiled, ate some more, and finally looked up at me and said with tears in his eyes, "Irma, in all my years as a neurologist, I have never witnessed anything like this." He too could not explain what happened. Finally, he said "It's a miracle."

I am grateful that my daughters grew up to be amazing young leaders who, despite their career paths, still give many volunteer hours alongside their daddy. Yes, my *sueno*, my dream, tells me that I am just getting started. Finally, I am able to share this news with you. My mixed feelings for sharing this good news was because I want this good news for all of my Familia Unida family and all of you who are living with an illness or disability. I pray for more miracles so that more continue to receive healing. I trust and do believe that this prayer has been answered, and, yes, miracles are happening all around us. I pray for a cure and more peace.

Some may say that I was misdiagnosed, while others may call this a miracle. I say that God and miracles are present every day, and I am committed more than ever to continue on my journey to share hugs, love, and ask that you do the same. With God's blessings, I will continue on this journey of service to many and will be traveling near and far, sharing acts of kindness, spreading love that is contagious, and I ask you to join me on this journey that is healing and the most wonderful feeling in the world. Yes, with you and me and others, we are...Simply Amor.

Thank you for reading my book, and I hope that our paths will cross some day, and if they don't, please create a path of wellness for yourself and don't ever stop believing in you! Remember that "You Are Not Alone" (*No Estas Solo*).

"Families united connected by hearts and love that have no color lines." MS has a new meaning to me. M and S stands for Miracles Soar.

Simply Amor,
Irma Resendez

Conclusion

$\mathcal{T}$he book cover of Juan and I traveling on his brand new motorcycle on the Santa Monica freeway takes me back to the summer of 1980 when we were dating. My daughter Johnnie Nicole found this photo of us in an old photo album that was put away in a box that hadn't been touched for years. The box contained photos of her daddy and I when we were dating in the early 1980's. Johnnie now in her late 20's claimed the photo once she found it and for several years the cover photo of Juan and I was displayed on Johnnie Nicole's refrigerator at her home secured by a magnet that kept those memories very much in our present and a reminder of young love.

How it seems like just yesterday that my sister Jackie was traveling in her car beside my mom who was seated in the front seat next to her. My mom captured this photo of us. We were going to all gather at the Santa Monica beach for lunch and a walk on the beach on this sunny summer day. A period in my life where love was new, innocence's was prevalent and I was a naïve young girl who had just turned twenty years old with no worries or fears. I felt the freedom to ride and was becoming familiar with the new emotions that told me I was in love. There was no helmet law back then. My hair was free in the wind and so was my spirit! Free from multiple sclerosis, not married yet. Marriage would happen four years later and Johnnie Nicole would be born two years after that and Jacqueline fifthteen months later.

What a beautiful thought to recall my mama excited to capture a photo of Juan and I as we traveled besides them with the breeze from the wind and a taste of the saltwater. My sister Jackie was looking over me nearby and close, similar to how we still look out for each other today. The years and life has happened so fast. Now Juan with his gray hair, and mine would be gray too if I didn't dye it dark brown every three weeks. My sister Jackie is now married and gave birth to her son and continues to be the other mother to my daughters. God bless my mom for hanging in there every year despite her aches and pains. She will be 80 years old soon.

My love for Juan continues to flourish and we still cuddle every night like we did that cold scary night that forever changed my path. Today, I have a renewed freedom and love for life like never before. I am excited to share so much more with you. I feel like I have been born again and given another opportunity to feel the freedom and desire to do much more for my community. I am ready to travel to many new places and meet many great people who I hope will be inspired to also share of their meaningful journey that will bring peace and love for self and others too. Please share your passion and peace will fill your heart.

CPSIA information can be obtained
at www.ICGtesting.com
Printed in the USA
LVOW13s1643190817
545627LV00035B/311/P